COMPANERAS

Voices from the
Latin American Women's Movement
Edited by Gaby Küppers

LATIN AMERICA
BUREAU

The Latin America Bureau is an independent research and publishing organisation. It works to broaden public understanding of issues of human rights and social and economic justice in Latin America and the Caribbean.

First published in the UK in April 1994 by the Latin America Bureau (Reseach and Action) Ltd, 1 Amwell Street, London EC1R 1UL

First published as *Feministamente* by Peter Hammer Verlag, Wuppertal, 1992

© (English language) Gaby Küppers

A CIP catalogue record for this book is available from the British Library

ISBN 0 906156 86 6 (pbk)
ISBN 0 906156 87 4 (hbk)

Editor: Helen Collinson

Cover photograph: Cuban women at a demonstration, Barry Lewis/Network
Cover design: Andy Dark

Printed by Russell Press, Nottingham NG7 3HN
Trade distribution in UK by Central Books, 99 Wallis Road, London E9 5LN
Distribution in North America by Monthly Review Press, 122 West 27th Street, New York, NY 10001

Contents

INTRODUCTION

In the interviews and articles which follow, Latin American and Caribbean women speak for themselves about their political activism. Their words pay tribute to the independent women's movements which have developed across the continent over the past twenty years and to the increasingly vocal assertion of women's demands within mainstream social movements. All the women included in this collection are politically active in one way or another: in popular organisations, political parties or autonomous feminist groups. They speak of a growing protagonism among women in Latin America and agree that in recent times sensitivity to women's issues has increased in the public consciousness of their respective countries. Jael Bueno from Bolivia goes as far as to say that 'no one wants to be a *machista* anymore.' Despite the different experiences of the women interviewed, common threads run through their conversations. Most stress that they are not fighting individual *machos* but the whole system of *machismo* which, often under the guise of neo-liberalism, excludes women, denies them opportunities and does them physical as well as emotional damage. *Machismo* can be conquered in many ways but rarely on an individual basis. There is unanimous agreement that race, class and sex are the decisive factors of our social existence and that a strategy is needed on all three fronts.

Across Latin America, feminists are criticised for acting like the female counterparts of *machismo* so women activists tend to treat the term 'feminism' with caution. They manage without it or introduce it gradually by example. Many define themselves as the 'female section' of popular organisations. Those who use the word, 'feminism', point out that it is not about women *per se* but about the relationship between the sexes. This relationship needs to be changed, not turned upside down.

A recurrent debate among Latin American feminists concerns the extent to which they should participate in social institutions and their relationship to power. In Mexico, for example, a broad-based feminist women's alliance was formed before the Mexican parliamentary elections in August 1991. By taking an active part in the election campaign and presenting candidates, the alliance was partly responsible for the controversial results, namely reduced support for the ruling PRI party. But participation in social institutions has not always been so positive. During the 1980s, the women's movement in Nicaragua attracted widespread attention in Europe, many of us hoping that after the Sandinista revolution the unobtainable in Europe would be achieved in Central America. The solidarity movement sustained our hopes for a long time but gradually we women in the movement started to raise our doubts. Even where revolutions had triumphed, the liberation of women seemed far from being the order of the day. For years, the Nicaraguan women's association, AMNLAE, saw itself chiefly as a vehicle for the transmission of Sandinista policies, not for the promotion of interests specific to women.

Of course, news about developments in Latin America's women's movements remains largely beyond our reach. Where can you read about the national and regional women's meetings taking place across Latin America or the six continental feminist meetings held since 1981? During the 1980s participation in the feminist meetings increased more than tenfold, from 250 in Bogotá, Colombia in 1981 to 3,000 in San Bernardo, Argentina in 1990, and yet we heard almost nothing about them. A stocktake of events in the first few months of 1992 showed just how much was going on in Latin America: National Nicaraguan Women's Meeting in January; Central American Refugees Meeting in Mexico in February; Central American Women's Meeting in Nicaragua in March. None of these events were even mentioned in our own mass media. It is far easier to get hold of an article about the daily lives of women in Latin America or about poverty or illiteracy. It seems that politicians working in aid and development have only recently 'discovered' women; hence the glut of articles largely by European journalists and academics on the subject. By contrast, I wanted to make women visible as politically organised and organising participants and let them describe the process in their own words.

Inevitably, these interviews are coloured by my own European attitudes, most obviously in the questions I asked the women and in my editing. While recognising this problem, I also believe that the interviews encouraged a positive exchange of ideas and experiences. The following articles and interviews were collected in the early 1990s, either in Latin America itself or during visits to Germany by Latin American women. The different thematic sections serve as an initial orientation, though many of the texts could appear under several of the headings. Some countries are well-represented, others not at all. Deciding where to draw the line is one of the most unpleasant tasks of an editor, but *Compañeras* is an open-ended collection. Essentially, it could not be anything else, for the women's movement will not stand still. 'We want (...) to develop ourselves further, to include everyone; we don't want to write definitions in stone, multiplicity pleases us, it enriches this movement.' (Proclamation of the First Meeting of Central American Women in March, 1992)

Gaby Küppers
1992

FOREWORD

When I emigrated from Argentina to Peru in the mid-1970s, my knowledge of feminist movements barely stretched beyond the typical stereotypes. In those days women's liberation was never mentioned in the political programmes of the political groups I was involved with. There was no doubt about the importance of women's participation in changing society - as 'wife, comrade and mother'- but something else was equally certain: the asexuality required of those who strove for recognition in politics. The less 'sex' a woman comrade had, the greater her chance of being trusted with the authority to make political decisions. Beyond this, there were two unsubtle models of femininity to choose from: the desirable figure of Eva Perón[1], the self-sacrificing martyr, or Victoria Ocampo[2], the embodiment of aristocratic rebellion. Not a trace of feminism.

Powerless between the opposing forces of militancy and pleasure, we political activists opted for self-denial. After all, pleasure was a bourgeois deformation: only when the people had satisfied their basic needs could one mention the right to feel pleasure. So we put off our desires for later and felt pretty guilty in those few moments when we did feel pleasure.

While I wrestled with these absurdities and tried to cope with my first experience of motherhood, a group of middle-class women arranged a meeting to protest against a beauty contest in the Peruvian capital, Lima. The moment when that handful of women took to the streets would become the starting point of a revolution which appeared in various forms in different capitals of Latin America throughout the seventies. 'The Return of the Witches' was the headline in Lima's daily newspapers about this sudden uprising of women.[3] A few years later, it was with some of these same women that I took the first steps towards grasping the uniqueness of women's struggle and the need for women to organise autonomously. So it was that the closed fist of political rebellion was replaced by the entwined hands which represented our own sex. We began to feel the little girl inside us, to encourage each other towards creativity and to take up the pen. It was a time of total change, of experiments, of losing our fear, of toying with anarchy, and breaking down old structures. We celebrated our desire which we had only just discovered. 'The personal is political' was our slogan at that time. Our power, courage and rage of those years finally climaxed in the first feminist meeting of Latin America and the Caribbean in 1981 in Bogotá, Colombia.

The first groups of the 1970s were formed at great personal cost. Their members had to endure the well-known criticisms of being lesbians and of destroying the great plan for the people by dividing the class struggle. They were ridiculed by their comrades and fellow fighters in the political parties and mocked by the media. Despite everything, they managed to overcome that wall of calumny and stood firm.

During the 1980s Latin American feminism started to break the media's silence on the subject: here and there newspapers, radio and even TV programmes began to appear.[4] For the first time resource centres, legal aid offices, participation and self-help programmes received financial support from the First World. Admittedly, working-class women were generally absent from all this, despite various campaigns to encourage their integration. The struggle for the legalisation and free availability of abortion (illegal in all Latin American countries except Cuba) and for free access to contraceptives, as well as opposition to massive sterilisation programmes, were the main concerns of the feminist groups.

Always a minority and always provocative, these groups remained the domain of the middle classes: academics, scholars, women in the media and artists. Their demands were aimed at publicising and changing the poor state of health suffered by the majority of working women, but *campesinas* and women from the poor neighbourhoods seemed indifferent to the efforts of their fellow women. Working-class women continued to participate in mixed political organisations where they made joint demands with the men, renouncing any demands of their own.

As the economic crisis of the late 1970s deepened, the International Monetary Fund imposed drastic measures to reduce state spending on health, education and food subsidies. In response, mothers in the poor neighbourhoods with sole responsibility for their households started to organise. Their aims were very different from those of the feminist movement: they fought for electricity and running water to be installed in their neighbourhoods and for milk for their children. They organised communal kitchens to eke out their paltry incomes. In so doing, they were sometimes accused of reinforcing the habitual role of woman as the nurturing mother, the 'backbone' of the family. Were there any similarities between these women's organisations and feminism? In 1980 the Alternative Congress of the Women's Decade in Copenhagen concluded that women's daily struggle for better education and health care is 'also' feminism. How wonderful! But the debate had only just begun.

On 30 April 1977, in the midst of Argentina's military dictatorship, a group of 14 women between the ages of forty and sixty gathered in the Plaza de Mayo opposite the presidential palace in Buenos Aires. Defying police and troops, they walked in a circle around the independence monument as a sign of their resistance. It was a gesture which would be repeated every week from that moment on and would touch the whole world. The women were mothers who wanted to know where the security forces had taken their children. Right up to the present day they continue to demand the truth, to search and to confront. It is a real paradox that a group of women, or, more accurately, mothers with families, and not exactly young women at that, should become the very foundations of revolt against the most powerful military dictatorship Argentina had ever witnessed.[5] The mothers turned the most traditional role in patriarchal society into a subversive one. When they demanded the return of their children alive and the punishment of the guilty, they challenged the governing bodies of organised society; namely the law, the political parties, the military and the Church. It was their desire for knowledge which broke the ranks of the ruling social order. In a continent rife with injustice, authoritarianism and repression, it was not long before similar organisations sprang up in other Latin American countries. The question is, are these human rights campaigners also feminists?

The First Latin American and Caribbean Feminist Meeting in Bogotá was raided by the police who accused those present of 'offences against propriety'. It was the first women's festival ever celebrated in the Colombian capital. Five further meetings have followed the Bogotá meeting, each with more enthusiasm and with more calls for feminist organisation. At the Fourth Feminist Meeting in Taxco, Mexico, the evident opposition between 'feminism' and the 'women's movement' took on almost baroque forms, when representatives from the continent's social groups tried to articulate what was specific to each of them. In the end more than a thousand women spoke and feminism was redefined as a result: to the question of gender were added the issues of race, sexual orientation, cultural differences, human rights, and our aspirations for a new society. The attendance of more than 3,000 women at the Fifth Meeting in San Bernardo, Argentina, in 1990, suggests that the movement has become very diverse.

After twenty years, it would be impossible to describe the feminist movement in Latin America and the Caribbean as something which can be reduced to a single common denominator. Quite the opposite: it is a movement in the plural and the search for an identity has given way to a whole range of identities.[6] Indeed, feminism means unity in diversity, the power to be many and different, to be separate and separately organised and politically active. It is like a landscape in a state of permanent change. This presents a challenge, because we are attempting to organise disorganisation, to contain what is unstructured, and at the same time to sort out representatives, committees, and address lists. However, it is important to retain the permanent renewal of the movement, and with it the desire to be and to become, the refusal to conform to any model, the ability to respond to women's demands for survival and for basic human rights, including the right to be at peace with oneself and the right to pleasure. By no means is pleasure at the end of the list of demands: it is implicit in all our actions, in our groups and our togetherness. It is the pleasure which grows from a sense that we are no longer alone. Never again.

Esther Andradi
1992

Since 1983 Esther Andradi, an Argentinian, has lived and worked in Berlin as a journalist, screenwriter and author. In 1978 she published one of the first books about women in a Latin American country, *Ser mujer en el Peru* (Being a woman in Peru), with Ana Maria Portugal, while in Lima where she lived in exile between 1975 and 1983.

Footnotes

[1] Popularly known as 'Evita' in Argentina. Wife of General Juan Domingo Perón who was president of Argentina from 1946 to 1955. In 1949, Perón made Evita the leader of the Peronist Women's Party. From a poor family herself, Evita received massive support from the Argentine working class.

[2] Publisher and editor of *Sur*, an Argentine literary magazine, during the Perón presidency. In the early 1950s Victoria was imprisoned for opposing Perón's totalitarian regime.

[3] On Tuesday, 10 April, 1973, the lead article on the first page of *Ultima Hora* was: 'These ugly demonstrators from four days ago should be invited to a meeting to acquaint them with the use of cologne, shampoo and hairdressing, to convince the fat ones of the need for a little sport and the thin ones of the need for some extra food... Women as fat as fridges and as thin as sanatorium patients went to war against harmony, soft curves, fine skin and the beauty of a few wonderful young women whose mortal sin is simply their youth and whose unforgivable crime it is to decorate life in such a way as to make the presence and existence of certain other women unbearable...' Quoted from, Ana Maria Portugal: *'Hacia una comprensión del feminismo en el Peru.'* Lima, Peru, 1978.

[4] With the exception of the Mexican newspaper *Fem*, which was launched in the early 1970s and still exists today, feminist journalism only began in the 1980s.

[5] Esther Andradi: 'The subversive power of motherliness', in: Dorfler, Gasiorowski de Andrade, Roper, Wuttke (ed.): '*... there are worlds between them'- Women's Study Projects in Africa, Asia and Latin America*, Saarbrucken 1988

[6] '... Therefore Juanita could say with pride: I am a Costa Rican, black, lesbian feminist and socialist...' Maria Moreno: *'Pluralismo de la diferencia'*, in *Sur*, 25/ 11/90, Buenos Aires, Argentina

AUTONOMY

Margarita Muñoz (Panama)

Fighting *machismo* and US intervention

Panama is the youngest country in Spanish-speaking Latin America. Until 1903 it formed the northernmost province of Colombia. It was separated from Colombia when the Colombian government refused to give the United States the concession to build a canal between the Pacific and the Atlantic through this area. After Panama's 'independence', US firms moved in to build the canal. On its completion in 1914 the US claimed sovereignty over the canal and the so-called canal zone, a strip of land five miles wide on each bank. As a consequence, the republic of Panama consists of two unconnected sections, between which an area of 1,640 square kilometres is governed by the US.

The military coup of 1968 which brought Omar Torrijos Herrera to power, was a turning point in Panama's development. Unlike the reactionary military regimes which seized power in most Latin American countries in the 1970s, Torrijos introduced a programme of limited social reforms and national independence. In 1977 a mass mobilisation of the population and an international publicity campaign, coinciding with a temporary change in US policy during the Carter era, enabled him to secure a revision of the canal treaty which established the return of the canal and the canal zone to Panama in 1999. In 1980 Omar Torrijos died in a mysterious plane crash.

During the Reagan presidency of the 1980s increasing numbers of US citizens spoke out against the return of the canal and the canal zone to Panama. There are various important US military installations in the canal zones, among them the US Forces' South command (Southcom). The US government's campaign against the Panamanian military chief, General Noriega, which began in 1987 has to be viewed against this background. It finally ended with US military intervention in Panama in December 1989, in which several thousand people (predominantly Panama's civilian population) lost their lives. What was at stake for the US was not the overthrow of a military involved in drug trafficking, but the guarantee of long-term US influence in a country of strategic importance by installing a compliant government in Panama.

The US policy of aggression towards Panama in the last few years has posed a dilemma for the Panamanian left-wing opposition, including the women's movement. Noriega's, or rather his puppets', dictatorial and corrupt regime was presented as the defender of national sovereignty against US domination. And yet the Left did not want to side with the General any more than they wanted to play into the hands of the US and its Panamanian acolytes. This dilemma paralysed the popular movement during 1988 and 1989. But after the US invasion it began to regroup and organised women played an important role in this, as Margarita Muñoz of Panama's *Coordinadora Nacional de la Mujer* (CNM), the National Women's Commission, explains.

* * * * * * * * * *

Margarita, you call yourself a feminist. What does feminism mean in Latin America?

To begin with, I think our definition of feminism in Latin America is different from yours in Europe. The first thing we Latin American women have to fight against is a system in which the rich oppress the poor. Bear in mind that the vast majority of women are poor. But, of course, we also have to fight against male repression which we call *machismo* and that involves taking on the whole social structure. Incidentally, it's not a struggle against 'the man at my side', as many people think. This double repression means we have two struggles on our hands and that's why we have feminist organisations.

What were your personal motives for becoming a feminist?

I think I was already a feminist in the way I analysed things long before I called myself one. Ever since I got married I'd experienced situations time and time again which I felt were unjust, like always being the first to get up in the morning and make breakfast for my husband without ever receiving a penny for it. Later on in the textile union I had to deal with the same vertical, *macho* structure. I'd reached one of the highest levels of the union hierarchy and had been elected the women's officer when I noticed that suddenly I no longer had just one boss (in other words, the one in my factory) but a whole team of bosses: the leader of the union and all the men on the executive of the union suddenly started treating me as their inferior. They had no respect for me anymore. I don't mean I wanted them to be all chivalrous because I'm not bothered about that. It's more that they didn't take me seriously. They didn't treat me as an equal. They tried to pick holes in my work and I always had to prepare more reports than the others.

Then there was the time when some of us wanted to find out why women didn't stand up for their rights, even when they were union members. So we organised a seminar which was open to all female union members, not just the ones in the leadership. We worked on proposals to include more women in the union and then we presented them to the union executive. Their response was to accuse us of sexism! They said we were trying to create a parallel union and creating divisions. Their reaction made it totally impossible to further women's rights in the union in any serious way.

Did you just accept this situation or did you fight against it?

Well, I came up through the union ranks not because I had a pretty face but because I was prepared to take responsibility for my proposals. I felt good about every step of the way then and always kept looking upwards. But there were still just two of us women in the leadership of the union and one day we noticed that our proposals for reforms were no longer well-received. People started to laugh at us and point their finger at us: 'Just look at them,' they'd tut. 'There they are clucking away together in the corner again!' It was wrong to think that in time the men would get bored of this game. If I said anything at all about women, you could bet your bottom dollar the men would joke about it. And there was no point in saying: 'I'd just like to know what's so funny. I'm not telling any jokes!'

In situations like that, isn't the best solution just to have done with it and get out?

At first, we decided against simply leaving the union because we could could benefit from the women's commission. Our male colleagues on the executive certainly had quite a keen interest in women in the union becoming politically active. They even chose the name of the commission; they called it the 'National Commission of Female Workers'. But as time went by, we realised that instead of slogging our guts out on behalf of women in the union, an organisation of women in the poor neighbourhoods - right there, where they lived - could be much more effective. At least that would overcome one problem: the women wouldn't have to put up with any more dirty looks from their husbands or partners for getting home late because of an after-work union meeting. It's still the rule here that the wife has to ask her husband's permission when she leaves the house. Women themselves often think it has to be like that.

So the results and recommendations of the women's seminars, the reaction of the union executive to these and, finally, the subordination of women members to the interests of the trade union, prompted us to begin working with women outside the factories, not just workers, but also housewives and women who were still in training, and the self-employed. So we founded the National Women's Commission (CNM), as an independent organisation. Of course we haven't entirely given up the work in the union, because we felt responsible for the women there.

The CNM was founded before the US invasion of Panama in December 1989. To what extent was your work influenced by the invation and what had changed since then?

Before the invasion we tried to point out the ways in which women were manipulated by the ruling party, the military, and the opposition parties. By the way, I also count the Communist Party as one of the ruling parties because it subscribes very closely to the government's views. The Communist Party was anti-imperialist, full stop. They didn't say a word about any of the internal problems facing the population, let alone the repression of women or the deterioration in healthcare. At that time the slogan 'Sovereignty and Nationalism' was bandied about by one side and 'Democracy' by the other. The rich women who opposed Noriega organised demonstrations as part of the so-called *Crusada Civilista* (Civil Crusade). They banged saucepans just as protesting women had done in Chile years before, but of course they weren't interested in the women (their maids, in other words) who later had to cook in those very same saucepans. Even the Catholic Church called for women to join in these demonstrations which they did in enormous numbers. We saw it as a sort of political prostitution of women, because it exploited women's traditional feelings of responsibility for feeding the family in a very hypocritical fashion.

For us as a small minority it was difficult to form alliances with the anti-imperialist groups, because we agreed with them on some points, but not on all. So we just tried to explain to the women in our own organisation about the politicial abuse which women were being subjected to. In our view, a woman is an active political subject, not an object to be manipulated for political ends. I know we're not perfect, but at least the women in our organisation have always opposed the invasion, both before and after. Straight after the invasion the CNM joined the Solidarity Committee founded at that time and was very active in it.

You've just criticised the attitude of the Communist Party at that time. What position did women in the Communist Party have? Were there disagreements between you? I'm referring to the constant debate as to whether there can be agreement between women beyond the limits of a political party or not.

There was one issue we were all agreed on and which for us in Panama is the most important thing of all: we were all for the nation of Panama and against the imperialism of the US. Apart from that, there were differences which corresponded to party lines: for the communists there were no internal problems in the country, all evil came from outside. And, incidentally, that's what's been spread abroad since President Torrijos' time. As regards women it means: women in Panama are fine, they have no problems. It was even a source of pride to declare that Panamanian women were more educated and more hardworking than the men. But no one ever mentioned the type of work women did. It was kept secret that they were forced to do work that was damaging to their health, that after their studies they couldn't find any suitable work, that they always drew the short straw in competition with men and that that was the case everywhere, even in the state-controlled authorities. None of the political parties close to the previous government ever dreamt of pointing this out. And it's mentioned even less today. Women in the ruling Christian Democrat party are all in league to subjugate women, as I would call it. Women should not attempt to imitate men or, even worse, outdo them, politically, ideologically or academically. The sad thing is that the women now in parliament literally described themselves as wearing spurs during the election campaign. We see spurs as a masculine symbol so, really, they're trying to practice politics like men. This contradiction between the ideal of the little woman on the one hand and their absorption of male characteristics on the other doesn't go down well with the women from the poor and working-class sectors. Women in the poor neighbourhoods think politics is a dirty business and they won't go near it unless they feel it's worthwhile.

On the other hand, isn't it also difficult for poor and working-class women to relate to you, when you call yourselves feminists?

In Panama there are quite a few other groups that also call themselves feminist. But in general it's restricted to intellectual circles. There's no way we can avoid shocking people when we step outside our own little circle (let's face it, we're no bigger than that), and describe ourselves as feminists. We often get the same reaction even from people who think of themselves as being ideologically advanced. We'll have to wait another century before some men stop feeling personally attacked. We're trying to explain this term, feminism, with our women as delicately as possible. We say that being a feminist doesn't mean burning bras, smoking like a chimney in the street, drinking hard spirits or refusing to have children. We make it clear that feminism doesn't oblige us to oppose our own cultural heritage. Until now women have been quite sympathetic to our point of view.

The invasion is undoubtedly the most significant moment in Panama's history in recent years. In retrospect, how has the invasion affected the work and standing of the different women's groups in Panama?

Even before the invasion, membership of the large women's organisations supported by the ruling parties was dwindling. These were traditionally outreach organisations for the political parties and their duties ranged from making coffee at political meetings to supporting election campaigns out on the streets. This way of organising is now out of date so they barely exist anymore. Meanwhile the three or four feminist groups are really very small groups who hand out a few magazines and mainly mix in intellectual circles.

It's hard for me to say this in view of the terrible things that happened, but the invasion actually had a positive effect on our group. We were very small beforehand. The invasion united women from the poor neighbourhoods because they were directly affected by the invasion. They certainly didn't approach us because they wanted to join a women's organisation or because they felt it was theoretically correct. Their motives were economic: they had to ensure their own survival. Of course we're not an organisation that provides charitable assistance. We don't have any bread to distribute, but we do have survival strategies to teach. So we set up production projects for women. The women we work with live in urban areas where there's very little infrastructure and it's quite easy to find common demands. These demands motivated them to take collective action to improve their situation.

Apart from the economic situation, what has changed for women since the invasion?

Economic and social concerns are very intertwined. Many women, like the men, have lost their jobs recently. The men have less chance of finding a new job so they often stay at home to look after the kids, while the women find a new job somewhere or other. As you can imagine, that makes the men feel very frustrated which they take out on the women and children by getting aggressive. So the abuse of women is increasing. At the same time women have to work harder and harder for less and less money, because there's no shortage of cheap women workers. For both these reasons women's health is deteriorating. They have almost no access to healthcare any more, either because it's ceased to exist or because it's far too expensive. The women have no choice but to unite and organise themselves. We're now trying to develop women's awareness of their great importance in society and their potential strength.

During the military invasion, Panama City was turned into a sort of giant barracks. What effect did this militarisation have on women?

At the time the saddest and most shaming thing for us was that many women approached the US soldiers and offered themselves as prostitutes. Some even had relationships with them. In a way, I think this behaviour was understandable because at first people were completely ignorant about the extent of the invading forces' carnage and destruction. But when the mass graves were found and it transpired that people had been tortured and whole districts razed to the ground, the soldiers were seen in a totaly different light. The situation has changed today in that the US soldiers only come out in force when they're making drug raids.

Wherever a state of war exists I tend to think of rape rather than prostitution. Did that also happen here?

Yes, it did. Women weren't only raped, they were also murdered. During the invasion many prisoners escaped from Modelo prison, including a lot of violent criminals.

How did they manage to escape?

Well, that's still a mystery. Modelo prison is practically opposite the barracks which the US troops destroyed. Some say it was Noriega's soldiers, others claim it was the US troops. Judge for yourself! Anyway, the end result was an increase in chaos which certain people found very useful at that point. Many of the escaped prisoners carried weapons with them. The US was certainly responsible for the fact that so many people in Panama managed to get hold of weapons. This brought the situation to boiling point. Let me give you an example of the sort of things that went on at that time. A taxi driver was stopped. The passenger, a woman, was dragged out of the car and the driver had to watch while the woman was raped and murdered. Not long ago ago one of my colleagues was mugged - she should be glad nothing worse happened to her!

Instead of catching the prisoners again and demanding compensation from the US, the newspapers lamented the lack of patrols. So now there are more and more private security services, which obviously only well-off people can afford. Doña Fulana can feel safe in her bed because there's a guard standing at her front door but it's a different matter for people like us... We only dare work in the poor neighbourhoods during daylight hours which severely limits the amount of work we can do because the distances we have to travel are quite large.

How many women belong to your organisation?

First I should say a few words about the structure of our organisation. We've set up what we call women's working groups. Of course, the participants aren't entered on any membership list because we realised they didn't want that. We tried that in the early days, but we never got more than eighteen names! Getting entered on a list is too much like the way political parties work. It's always been the custom for political parties to give out five pounds of rice or a bottle of cooking oil when someone joins up. So it's quite common to meet a woman with five different party memberships. In people's minds membership has more to do with food than with support for a political manifesto! So women who join us are sort of 'free associates'. They don't need to sign any CNM papers.

But if we're talking numbers; between ten and fifteen women belong to each main working group, of which we have four in the capital and a few in the provinces. That gives a total of about eighty women. These women then act as disseminators in their own areas so that our radius of action extends far beyond each group. The basic aim of the working groups is to raise consciousness but also to provide training in things like health education. The women can then go out and approach fifty, a hundred or even two hundred more interested people in their local areas.

Let's take an example of a place where there's no running water. Our women light the first sparks, so to speak, because they know where to begin, that you have to go to the Ministry of Health and the Water Authority. They set the campaign for running water in motion. By doing this they've mobilised the women without actually solving the problem for them. Men often join in as well and suddenly you've mobilised 600 people!

At this point I should mention that we're in favour of coooperation with other women's groups and organisations, wherever possible. For example, there was once an initiative to get an institute named after a famous feminist pioneer in Panama. The idea came from the women in a Trotskyist group. We had no problem in joining the initiative because they were right. Why should our pioneers be consigned to oblivion? But alliances aren't always easy. More often than not they fall apart. Unfortunately, new alliances are formed very rarely. Everyone just goes home on their own and that's the end of it!

How do you see yourselves in the Latin American context? Do you feel well integrated at a continental level?

No, we feel quite isolated. The former government policy of presenting a rosy picture of the position of Panamanian women dies hard. It's absurd! If it were true, we'd certainly be the only women in Latin America who were doing all right. But CNM has a lot of contact with foreign women's organisations who haven't swallowed this rubbish. The difficulties crop up when there's talk of the Panamanian people as a whole. Certainly governments like Nicaragua's Sandinista government, for example, or Cuba's, have expressed their views about Panama's situation, but no one really takes into account that there's also a population in our country. Do you know, we were invited to the First Meeting of Central American Women where, as usual, the national anthems of the Central American countries were played - but only five anthems. Panama was simply forgotten!

It sounds like you're feeling misjudged, misunderstood or simply over-looked? Is that right?

I think there's a lot of ignorance about. The fact that we're independent with no sister organisations in other countries mobilising on our behalf doesn't make it any easier. We still have a lot to do.

Jael Bueno (Bolivia)

'No one wants to be *machista* anymore.' The rise of Bolivian feminism

First came the Spanish colonisers, then British and North American enterprises. Their common aim was to exploit Bolivia's natural resources, particularly tin and silver, at the expense of the indigenous population. The popular revolution of 1952 was a response to this exploitation and in its wake Bolivian workers formed powerful trade unions to try and improve their miserable working and living conditions. From 1952 until 1985 the *Central Obrera Boliviana (COB),* the Bolivian Trades Union Congress, wielded greater influence over national political life than any other Latin America trade union movement, even after the 1964 military coup put a definitive end to the revolutionary period. Throughout the 1970s and 1980s tin miners' wives' committees played a decisive role in the political struggles against the military dictatorship. With the publication of the book, *Let Me Speak* by the Bolivian miner's wife, Domitila Barrios de Chungara, their actions became world famous.

The crash of the world tin price in 1985 destroyed Bolivia's mining industry and with it, the influential bargaining position of the trade unions. It also prompted the government to adopt a free-market 'shock treatment': deregulation of prices, elimination of subsidies and price supports, and the dismantling of state enterprises. Virtually overnight this neoliberal onslaught put an end to inflation and thrust the state's deficit-ridden accounts into the black. But at a price: health and education budgets have been slashed; thousands of workers have been laid off while an influx of cheap food imports have made farming unprofitable.

In the scramble to survive, thousands of Bolivian women are turning to the so-called 'informal sector' to work as street vendors, market sellers, or in tiny, family-run workshops. Large numbers of women are now earning an income for the first time in their lives, but without any protection, price supports, or job security. A large proportion of Bolivian women are single parents with sole responsibility for the upbringing of their children.

In the following contribution, Jael Bueno describes the organisation of

Bolivian women in the context of this struggle for survival. She is a sociologist and a co-worker at the *Centro de Estudios y Trabajo de la Mujer (CETM)*, Women's Studies and Employment Centre, in the Bolivian city of Cochabamba. The centre gives advice to women and also works with prostitutes.

* * * * * * * * * *

Jael, when did the women's movement and feminism become an issue in Bolivia?

Not that long ago. Since 1985, to be more precise, because that was an important year for women worldwide (the end of the UN Women's Decade). At first there were just a handful of small non-governmental organisations (NGOs) working exclusively on women's issues .

Did the impulse for that come from abroad?

No, it wasn't quite like that. Basically the initiative came from the women who went to the First and Second Latin America and Caribbean Feminist Meetings in the early eighties and were motivated to take up the cause of women. It wasn't possible to do this in any of the existing organisations, partly because of *machismo* and partly because the structures of these organisations weren't suited to it. So the women I've just mentioned decided to create their own space.

What sort of women were they on the whole?

Middle-class women and students mainly, plus a few teachers and university lecturers. In La Paz they founded the *Centro de Información y Documentación para la Mujer (CIDEM)*, Women's Information and Documentation Centre, and *Gregoria Apaza* which promoted various production projects. In Santa Cruz they set up the *Foro de la Mujer*, Women's Forum, which now has a daily morning radio programme for women and in Cochabamba the CETM, where I work. They've all tried to work with existing women's organisations like the Mothers' Centres organised by Caritas (a Catholic charity) which you'll find all over Bolivia. The Mothers' Centres receive food from Europe and the US and the mothers meet once a week to knit or make handicrafts of some sort. The new women's centres I've just mentioned have used existing groups like the mother's centres to get discussion going on issues specific to women.

Feminism will spread if we can influence the structures that already exist for women. In this way it won't just be the domain of intellectual groups. That's what's positive. I think we're creating a sort of social utopia quite instinctively. You see, women in the mothers' centres don't just make individual demands for their own personal development; they also make social ones. And that's exactly what our country needs. As you know, in Bolivia as in other Latin American countries, conflicts of a gender-specific nature overlap with conflicts about class and race.

In Cochabamba you're involved in the publication of a women's magazine. How long have your been publishing this magazine and how successful has it been?

It's produced by the CETM which was founded in 1986 by a group of us who'd done women's studies at university. We started publishing a newspaper supplement called *Nosotras* (the female form of 'we') which we managed to include in *Hoy* (Today), a local daily newspaper in Cochabamba. In 1990 we made a deal to publish a supplement in the weekly newspaper, *Aqui* (Here), in La Paz . This also appears in the monthly paper *Lawray* (Sparks). So there are now two free feminist newspaper supplements in Bolivia with a national circulation.

You said feminist newspaper supplements...

Yes, that's right. They're explicitly feminist, not just feminine in the classic sense of women's magazines.

Is that an acceptable term in Bolivia today?

At first it was pretty difficult to describe oneself or, indeed, anything as being feminist - just like it was elsewhere. All the slanders under the sun rained down on us. But it's simply a question of consciousness-raising, right? You have to think of feminism as a way of life, not as a kind of empty debate which would never sustain any of us. For us, feminism means changing our lives and our attitudes, but also our relationships with women as well as with men - in fact, with everyone around us.

What's it really like, then, for you women on the magazine? What kind of relationships do you have?

Obviously we'd all had the usual relationships. And that's exactly where our struggle began. We tried to change our relationships with our *compañeros*. You can imagine that's not easy in a world where the population is fifty per cent male, and most men are *machistas*.

Your compañero *and your personal struggles are one thing but it's another thing to win approval and trust from women who've been party to the usual devaluing stereotypes about feminism all their lives.*

As I said, feminism is a way of life. Obviously you can't sound off about feminism and at the same time keep a maid at home. It's true that words like *comehombres* (man-eaters) get banded about in Cochabamba and La Paz, but I'm not sure whether women involved in the projects we've set up really find it difficult to relate to feminists. In fact, I think that in the last few years feminists have managed to influence popular attitudes. You'd be surprised, but in the bars of Cochabamba today, you often hear men say, 'Well, as for me, I'm no *machista*.'

Why do these men feel personally attacked?

They've heard their *compañeras* talk about *machismo* as something negative and feminism's been discussed quite a lot here recently.

Going back to your magazine again, what's its circulation?

5,000.

I imagine it must be very difficult for a magazine like yours to reach indigenous women - in other words, the majority of women in Bolivia. Besides, many of them can't even read.

Well, often the magazine is read out by the leaders of women's groups. Then the contents of the articles which interest them are incorporated into the group's work. Let's take an obvious example - an article about 'What is feminism?'. At a meeting the group leader might ask the *campesinas* who've turned up for their opinion on the subject and then working groups are formed on the basis of their responses. Or if you want to talk about violence, then first of all you ask each woman to comment on the issue. The task of the group leader is then to collate all the opinions voiced and translate them into the work of the group.

In conversation with other Latin American women, for example, at the Fifth Latin America and Caribbean feminist meeting, have you got the impression that the situation for women and feminism is more or less the same elsewhere or could you describe something that's typically Bolivian?

I do think there's something typically Bolivian about our feminism. Our own culture plays a very important role, just as it does in Peru and Ecuador. In these three countries the indigenous population wasn't massacred during the Spanish conquest and the presence of indigenous women has a strong influence on our thinking. In Bolivia, for example, there's a national organisation of *campesinas*, the *Federación Nacional Bartolina Sisa*. The name comes from an Aymara woman who fought against the Spanish long ago. The women of *Bartolina Sisa* are particularly concerned about the relationship between men and women and have introduced a gender-specific perspective on this. They argue that the world used to be more harmonious because men and women were on an equal footing. Today there's no longer this equality, this balance. To unite all our forces once again in the struggle for a better world and to be effective as men and women working together, the women from *Bartolina Sisa* say the old balance must be re-instated. We women must regain our rights, we must speak with the same energy and the same confidence as men. And we must introduce our own demands into the general demands of our people. In my opinion that is the most obvious characteristic of feminism in Bolivia.

For those of us in Europe who began to get interested in the situation of Latin American women a few years ago, Domitila, the miner's wife from Siglo XX, was particularly inspiring. In her book, Let Me Speak, *she said a lot of very important things about women's struggle in Latin America. Now that the great Bolivian mining companies don't exist anymore, the miners' unions have lost their earlier influence. What's left now?*

Undoubtedly, the current economic policies are fatal for whole sectors of the population. But at least one thing has become clear through the demise of the unions. The reality in Bolivia is quite different from the way it was seen in a strictly Marxist sense whereby our whole society was divided into workers on the one hand and middle classes on the other. In fact, Bolivia mainly consists of indigenous *campesinos*. Austerity measures led to the dismissal of 5,000 workers in the mines. It turned out that the so-called vanguard, the workers in other words, weren't a vanguard at all, because many of the social conflicts affecting the country were excluded from its agenda. Today new agents for social change have appeared on the scene, such as the youth and women's organisations in the poor neighbourhoods who've got together to form advice centres, cultural centres and soup kitchens. Their answer to the economic crisis is: organise!

The miners' wives movement in the seventies was very important. For a start they succeeded in bringing back democracy to Bolivia. A handful of crazy women called a dictator to account and demanded democracy for the country. These women were the wives of miners and behaved as such, as 'wives of'. When the mining proletariat broke up, their organisation also broke up. But many of these women are now working in local women's organisations.

You yourself have a university background and work in a feminist study centre. Where do you think most is done for the women's movement and feminism? Isn't it in your own sector?

No, I think the poor and working classes do the most, because that's where you find the highest levels of conflict and so that's also where you'll find the greatest stimulus for the women.

Jael, you present quite an optimistic picture of activity and organisation at a time when pessimism is the order of the day everywhere and mass organisations are being replaced by various splinter groups. How do your views fit into this scenario?

Obviously the economic crisis which exists in all Latin American countries as well as Bolivia has made people less and less inclined to mobilise. When the dictatorships ended, organisations also began to disappear, as if suddenly there was no one to fight against anymore. The common enemy had disappeared.

But of course today there's another strong enemy; hunger, a hunger which claims its victims on a daily basis. It's the women who have to feed their families every day and so it's women who've become politically active on this issue to seek solutions. Everywhere you go in the poor neighbourhoods of Cochabamba and La Paz you'll see little enterprises where women are making handicrafts and trying to sell them. There are street vendors uniting to protect themselves against assault and washerwomen making joint demands for public laundries. I'm very optimistic in the sense that the ideological myths about the workers' vanguard which used to hinder our progress are becoming obsolete and are disappearing. In Bolivia for a long time people only talked about the workers. The situation in the poor neighbourhoods or the lot of the peasants in the east, who were being massacred by the landowners, was completely ingored. People never used to talk about the migration of rural people to the cities or the problems facing marginalised people.

On 11 October, 1990, Bolivian Women's Day, you proposed a motion in Parliament for the prosecution of sex crimes. This motion was accompanied by a petition with more than 20,000 signatures. How did you organise this?

We've created a co-ordinating committee called the *Plataforma de la Mujer*, Women's Platform, for all the NGOs working with women. The aim of this platform is to promote women's rights. Under our penal code there was no prosecution for rape, as long as the victim in question wasn't a minor or a virgin. In collaboration with women lawyers the platform has now prepared a parliamentary bill, calling on the government to end this impunity. Essentially, we're demanding that rape should no longer be regarded as a private matter between a man and a woman, but should be declared a crime against the physical and mental integrity of the victim and worthy of prosecution. If you look at the situation for a rape victim as it stands at the moment, the state won't instigate any legal proceedings whatsoever. So if a woman reports the crime and the rapist disputes it, there's no opportunity for proving the opposite with witnesses and convicting the rapist. If the act has caused a public outcry, then at best the rapist pays the victim a sort of hush-money and that's it.

Before we presented our bill, we ran a national campaign to raise awareness about the problem of rape. We had TV spots, leaflets and newspaper ads. Rape is not just a problem for the victim, it's a social problem. We think it's very important that sexuality is seen from the position that women are subjects, not objects.

Who did you ask to support the draft bill in Parliament?

We approached all the parties, from left to right.

Were the reactions different depending on their political allegiances?

No. In this respect, men are all the same.

Yance Urbina (El Salvador)

Building a feminist organisation inside the social movement.

From 1980 until January 1992 El Salvador was ravaged by civil war: on one side there were the security forces financed and trained by the US and supported by the country's powerful business and coffee elite; on the other the *Frente Farabundo Martí para la Liberación Nacional* (FMLN), the Farabundo Martí liberation movement, whose base of support came largely from rural peasants. In the early 1980s the Salvadorean military unleashed a massive wave of repression, with death-squad assassinations of popular leaders (including Archbishop Romero) and aerial bombardments of civilian communities. It failed to defeat the FMLN.

In search of a new strategy to neutralise the guerrillas, US advisors persuaded the Salvadorean government to create a limited, 'democratic opening'. Although selective repression against popular organisations continued, the civilian opposition used this opening to articulate their demands for democracy, prosecution of the uniformed murderers and torturers and a redistribution of property - particularly agricultural land. Women's groups voiced their demands alongside the trade unions, grassroots Christian movements, organisations of refugees and displaced people, co-operatives and student organisations. The upsurge in popular activism culminated in the National Debate for Peace in 1988 in which sixty organisations participated. Only the private-sector elite boycotted the session.

A renewed wave of repression in 1989 hit the popular movement once again but despite the closing of political space, most popular movement leaders remained determined to build the country's unarmed popular movement. Meanwhile the momentum for finding a peaceful solution to the conflict gathered pace, following the end of both the Contra War in Nicaragua and the Cold War at a global level. On 1 February 1992 the historic peace accords were signed between Salvadorean President Alfredo Cristiani and Comandante Leonel González of the FMLN.

Throughout the 1980s all civilian opposition groups were the victims of repression and state terror. To justify their violence against the civilian opposition, the government and the military repeatedly asserted that these groups were FMLN front organisations. Not wishing to add grist to the military's mill, popular organisations - women's organisations included - made no public mention of their close contact or relations with FMLN organisations, but after the signing of the peace accords a much more open discussion ensued about the relationship between the political parties and the various popular movements in El Salvador.

CONAMUS (National Co-ordinating Committee of Women in El Salvador), founded in 1986, pioneered a new type of women's organisation in Central America, with an emphasis on women's specific interests above all. CONAMUS's projects include a women's clinic, a women's refuge with 14 places and a weekly 15-minute radio programme produced by girls and young women between the ages of 17 and 20. The following interview with Yance Urbina, a co-worker from CONAMUS, was conducted in March 1991, several months before the signing of the peace accords. She talks about recent developments in El Salvador's women's movement on the eve of the accords.

* * * * * * * * * *

CONAMUS is the oldest of the new Salvadorean women's organisations, so to speak. Have the organisation's aims changed over the years?

No, the aims are the same. What's changed is the type of work we do because we've built up different areas of work. Our priority has always been the advancement and education of Salvadorean women. We try to raise consciousness about the problems we have as women and problems arising from the specific situation in El Salvador. This consciousness-raising is not an end in itself; it's a prerequisite for actively coming to grips with our problems.

Since November 1990 you've been publishing a magazine called Palabra de Mujer *(Women's Word). The sub-title says explicitly: 'Feminist Publication'. Were there discussions about this in your women's organisation?*

Oh yes, there were pretty lengthy discussions about this project, from the title of the magazine, right down to the finer details of production. But the result is that the magazine today is based on the consensus of all CONAMUS women. The name *Palabra de Mujer* has been carefully chosen. In our country if you want to stress the seriousness or reliability of a promise or a statement, you normally say: *'palabra de hombre que si'* (approximately:

'word of honour', literally: 'the word of a man'). We've put our own feminine word of honour in its place. 'Woman's Word' has exactly the same validity as any 'man's word'.

As regards the sub-heading, when we call our publication 'feminist', we're stating that it's much more open and goes much further than anything we've published before. *Palabra de Mujer* sees itself as a forum for discussion in which questioning and debate by CONAMUS is given equal space to contributions from women who aren't members of our organisation and women in other parts of Latin America or in Europe.

So describing your magazine as 'feminist' wasn't a stumbling block?

For some years now CONAMUS has had an internal debate about the description 'feminist', not just in relation to the magazine, but also in relation to our organisation as a whole. The time has come to call ourselves feminist.

How has the relationship between CONAMUS women, who describe themselves as feminist, and women from the poor and working classed developed? Have you met with support or caution?

There's been no open rejection whatsoever. I mean, if we take the magazine as a barometer of acceptance of feminism, *Palabra de Mujer* sold like hot cakes when it first came out. If poor and working-class women couldn't read it, it was read out to them by local CONAMUS activists and then discussed. The only clashes were with extremely traditional, *macho* attitudes. But generally there were no conflicts with the women we worked with, quite the opposite. I wouldn't want to suggest that was the end of the matter. Who knows what we may still provoke! Basically, we're in a transitional phase. The public support we've seen for feminism, refected in the magazine among other things, is still quite recent. We were ready to take this step so we did. At least there's now a close link between our praxis, our theoretical stance and our demands.

You've gone public with the magazine, so to speak, and shown your true colours. But you've also put yourselves on the frontline with T-shirts saying: 'Soy Feminista' (I am a feminist).

Yes, the T-shirts, like the magazine, are supposed to make our position clear to the outside world. As you might expect, reactions have varied: our male colleagues from the popular movements were quite surprised. Some thought that saying 'I'm a feminist' was the same as saying: 'I'm a *machista*'. Obviously we have to counter this with convincing arguments and avoid getting sarcastic like many of our critics. Every jibe at us also gives us an opportunity for discussion. Usually it transpires that the stupid things said about us have little substance and are simply prompted by prejudice.

Do you regard yourselves as a vanguard or does the existence of CONAMUS reflect the rise of more progressive attitudes among popular movements in El Salvador as a whole?

As far as feminism is concerned, CONAMUS is certainly one of the pioneering organisations. We're the only organisation that publishes a feminist magazine and openly calls itself feminist, the only one that has set up projects like a women's clinic and a women's refuge. Our experience over the last few years has made us push back the frontiers. There's also our grassroots work which has enabled us to expand enormously. We've been given strong support for our methods. We're not simply some little group that critically analyses society anymore. These days we represent a lot of women. Nevertheless, I'd prefer not to use the term, 'vanguard'. It sounds so presumptuous, as if we were the best and the most progressive.

Recently there've been indications of a change of heart inside the FMLN. It seems as if women's demands are getting more of an audience. What's your view on this?

I genuinely believe that CONAMUS' ideas have influenced a lot of different sectors. There's more discussion on all levels - and that in itself is a big success. New groups have grown out of CONAMUS. Our ideas for working on behalf of women stand as a precedent, really, and as a result of our initiatives, many issues have been seen as a problem for the first time. Since you're asking about the FMLN, it works underground, so it's not possible to have contact with FMLN people just like that. But actually it's clear that the FMLN has adopted the demands of women in the popular movements. To give you an example; in October, 1990 the FMLN made known their demands for a women's ministry which shows that the FMLN is at least concerned about women's issues. In my opinion it's also a product of women's pressure inside the FMLN.

The ARENA government also created a Departamento de la Mujer. *Was this established to take the wind out of your sails? Did they try and steal your arguments?*

No, not at all. The *Departamento* was set up at the National Families' Secretariat which doesn't have ministry status. They used it as a band-aid job on the worst sores. For example, in theory there should now be a doctor and a female psychologist in every health centre for the care of rape victims.

But, in so far as any medical assistance like that exists at all, it bears almost no resemblence to our approach because in the minds of the health workers staffing the clinics, the traditional image of women dies hard.

There was another thing they wanted to copy from us; the *Comités de Crédito Solidario* (Solidarity Credit Committees) which distributed small government cash loans. They mainly promoted these loan committees in poor neighbourhoods to pull the carpet out from under our feet. But the difference is that although the government can obviously offer much larger amounts of credit than us, they also demand much higher rates of interest. And when they grant a loan, they never provide any accompanying training programme like we do. We only demand a minimal rate of interest to give women the chance to make a go of it for longer periods of time. The loan is supposed to provide people with a viable survival strategy. But the state loans simply divert the economic crisis from the worst spots temporarily. Our plans for addressing problems specific to women don't interest them at all.

I could say similar things about other projects of theirs, especially as regards the media and propaganda, like their action on the pending family legislation which doesn't yet exist in El Salvador. What we've heard from them so far is a million miles from our own ideas. There was no public debate at all, no consultation with women or anything like that - just a draft bill which was presented by one of the commissions appointed by the Families' Secretariat. We regard this as a cosmetic attempt to create an image of a government that cares about the good of Salvadorean women. All they're really bothered about is patching things up in a superficial way while they let much more deep-seated problems just fester.

Do you think women are taken in by these con tricks?

There may well be some women who are taken in at first. But I'm sure they're wise to the government's real intentions. Political manipulation tends to be the hallmark of all government initiatives. People in El Salvador are no fools. They've certainly got enough sense to see the real agenda behind state projects.

CONAMUS is critical of the methods of the National Families' Secretariat. We don't think it's brought about any improvements for women because it doesn't address the real causes of the problem, like the entire economic structure, for example! As I've said, everything's just been patched up in a makeshift way.

As a women's organisation you also get involved in mainstream political campaigns, for example, in May 1990, when 62 women's organisations got together to form a platform for the national debate on the future political and economic organisation of the country. Can you say more about this process?

The initiative came from CONAMUS. We called it the *Concertación Nacional de Mujeres para la Paz y la Democracia* (National Women's Forum for Peace and Democracy). Its main aim was to collate the opinions of representatives from 62 women's organisations in El Salvador - organisations of *campesinas*, housewives, domestic servants, women from co-operatives, market traders, women from every possible sector. We asked them which issues they thought should be raised and what they thought about some of the points which had already been raised. Our initiative was a great success. We then ratified the document we'd drawn up in the presence of 400 representatives of 62 organisations. We passed on this document to the President, the FMLN, the UN and the *Comité Permanente del Debate Nacional* (Permanent Committee on the National Debate). In this way we managed to gain a platform for women far beyond CONAMUS itself. It was a collective achievement of all of us who'd signed the document. We sent it off to the respective parties, asking for it to be discussed. The government never responded and the UN fobbed us off. They just sent a sort of proof of receipt with a vague promise that they'd discuss it. Only the FMLN indicated that they wanted to have a discussion with us but this was obviously very difficult because they operate underground.

What were the main points in your document?

It clarified our position on demilitarisation, human rights, the future socio-economic structure of the country, our demand for legislation on the prosecution of rape and abuse, and changes in the penal and civil codes. We also demanded the abolition of conscription. Basically, we concentrated on issues which we felt provided practical solutions to the Salvadorean conflict.

You've just cited militarisation and violence against women as central problems. Some time ago you opened a women's refuge to help the victims of violence in a more direct way...

Violence in El Salvador affects everyone. There's a basic connection between military presence and violence against women. There are many cases of rape by members of the security forces, especially in the poor neighbourhoods. The military's impunity encourages this type of aggression against the civilian population. In El Salvador many soldiers roam about the country with weapons, even when they're on leave. Time and time again women and children die because the hand grenade of a soldier in the street suddenly goes off. We also know of many examples of violence by members of the military against their own wives.

The women's refuge came out of our experience with the battered women we treat at our clinic. Some of them don't want to go back home and for others it's not advisable because it means exposing themselves once again to a violent situation. Sometimes just seeing the street where they were raped can be sheer trauma for women.

On average how long do the women stay at the refuge?

All the women know right from the start that they can only stay there temporarily. We try and encourage awareness among the women that only they can find an alternative and they are the ones who must take responsibility for their future. CONAMUS can only be a support, we can't take the initiative away from the women.

I know you've visited women's refuges in Germany. Did you find any differences between them and the CONAMUS refuge?

Yes. For a start, the length of stay is much longer than at our refuge. I've heard that in Germany women sometimes stay in refuges for as long as three years. As far as we're concerned, the women's refuge isn't alternative accommodation, it's a springboard to venture out into life again, to clarify things away from one's usual surroundings.

And when you compare women's groups in Germany with yourselves in El Salvador, what differences or similarities have struck you most?

There are quite a few differences. We see ourselves as outreach organisations trying to involve more and more women. We have a gender-specific starting point which influences our political interventions in the mainstream. In Germany I only saw small groups. They seemed to be interested in nothing but themselves and had no intention of expanding. Also men can't participate in these groups in Germany. But here there are times when men are specifically allowed to be present at our events. Obviously there are also similarities, for example, in relation to violence against women. You also have women's refuges and advice centres. As far as feminist theory is concerned, we've certainly learnt a great deal from each other over the years. But even if we sometimes come to different conclusions, the exchange of ideas is still important.

Alba de Mejía (Honduras)

Demanding women's rights in the shadow of the military

During the 1980s the US transformed the small Central American republic of Honduras into their most important military stronghold in the region. Honduras was the scene of frequent large-scale military manoeuvres with massive participation by US forces, designed to bully the Sandinista government in Nicaragua and the popular movement in El Salvador. Honduras was also the logistical base and withdrawal zone for the anti-Sandinista Contras, equipped and financed by the US. From here they led their 'dirty war' against Nicaragua until 1990.

For the popular movement in Honduras the struggle against the the transformation of the country into a quasi US military colony has taken priority. This is also true of the women's movement which has had to deal with a spate of violence as a result of the country's militarisation alongside the 'routine' violence against women.

In 1990, Alba de Mejía of the *Visitación Padilla* (Women's Liberation Committee) came to Europe to make contact with European women's movements and solidarity movements and publicise the work of this anti-military women's organisation.

* * * * * * * * * *

What does your organisation do and what are its aims?

We work on three different levels. On one level we fight against the US military occupation of Honduras. The US has used Honduras as a military base since 1979 in order to hinder the general revolutionary process in Central America. They hold manoeuvres, install radar and so on... Around 80,000 North American soldiers have been in Honduras over the last ten years and this year (1990) there will be about 20,000. On another level we're committed to social justice and the liberation of women. In Honduras some eighty per cent of the population lives in poverty. Thirty-five per cent of the budget is spent on the payment of foreign debts and a further 35 per cent is spent on the upkeep of the national army. This leaves almost nothing for the basic needs of the people. Women are affected the most by this; something like 68 per cent of women and 72 per cent of children are malnourished. Women also suffer a great deal of violence from men; eight out of ten Honduran women admitted in an inquiry that they had been beaten by men at some time. And women still have no right to own property; meanwhile rape is regarded as merely an attack on a woman's honour, not a crime against her life and integrity. So we're demanding changes in the law.

Could you say more about the work you do?

We run training sessions for women on things like the connection between international debt and their own poverty. We also try to ensure that they become aware of their rights, the right to be in charge of their own bodies and the right to organise. So we've also set up a section in our office which offers legal and psychological advice.

We put up publicity posters in the three main cities in Honduras showing the effects of the military occupation. One of the worst consequences of the occupation is to do with health: Honduras has the highest rate of AIDS in Central America and it was the North American soldiers who brought AIDS into the country. The Honduran authorities don't even test them for AIDS. There's also been a sharp increase in prostitution in the areas around the military bases and there's a whole prostitution racket run by the corrupt Honduran military. They've got groups who go hunting for virgins for the *gringos*.

We also mobilise people for the three annual women's demonstrations. We're currently involved in building a technical school for women from the poor neighbourhoods to learn basic electrical skills. We also have workshops were women can learn men's tailoring. It's still just a small enterprise, but with the help of European women we would love to expand it, so that more women can become self-reliant and independent of men. In the cities we show women how to make food from soya. Because of rising inflation only 32 per cent of the population can afford red beans at the moment, even though they're a basic staple food. We also have a library which is mainly used by students and teachers. Forty-one per cent of women are illiterate so unfortunately it's rarely used by the poor. In one very poor neighbourhood we've set up a kindergarten for twenty children and the women are in the process of founding a co-operative to teach all the children in the neighbourhood.

As women who are organised, have you been the targets of repression?

Yes, we have. The police keep a constant watch over our office; they take photographs of the demonstrations and keep tabs on us all. They've also phoned me at home and threatened to kill me. So, yes, our organisation is harassed a great deal by the police and we want European women to know that and protest to our government. Because in our struggle for the rights of women and the poor we cannot afford to lose a single woman through police aggression.

Has repression increased since the change in government?

We think of our organisation as a sort of barometer of the level of repression. In March a colleague was arrested by the police. They interrogated her about the activities of the committee and threatened her. The repression in this country is selective, it's not directed against everyone, but against the representatives of popular organisations and trade unions. A hundred and fifty people 'disappeared' in Honduras between 1980 and 1984, many have been unjustly imprisoned, tortured or have gone into exile because they received death threats, some as recently as last year and this year...

In Honduras there are also mixed organisations fighting against the military occupation and for social justice. As a women's organisation, are your politics different from theirs?

Well, we think of power in very broad terms. We believe that power is expressed just as much in personal relationships as it is in the relationship of the social classes to one another. For us, what happens in the bedroom is also politics. We have to fight on lots of different fronts. At the moment we're suffering a military occupation but at the same time there's violence at home. Both of them co-exist and it's all part of the same thing. You can't just sit back and wait for the revolution. Progressive men in Honduras will say; first the revolution and then the liberation of women, as if the revolution would liberate women from their 14 hours of housework.

Are you supported by mixed organisations then?

Yes, we're in touch with other organisations and are also represented on the board of an umbrella group for various popular organisations, but we have a good deal of autonomy. Sometimes we work with groups that are headed by men but we conduct all the committee's affairs ourselves. Whenever men help us with certain things we're the ones who decide how they should be done.

Do you have any contact with other women's organisations in Central America?

Naturally we're in contact with women in Guatemala, El Salvador, Nicaragua and Costa Rica. Last year we held a Central American Women's Conference to celebrate the second anniversary of the Esquipulas peace treaty. Since this meeting in Guatemala we've approached many, many organisations in Central America about founding the Permanent Assembly of Central American Women for Peace. This year we're going to meet in El Salvador, in August again, on the anniversary of Esquipulas.[1] It's always the same issues because at the end of the day even if people weren't dying from bullets anymore, in our part of the world they'd go on dying from malnutrition and a lack of solidarity. If there isn't even a minimum standard of living, then society gives no support to those who have the least means, so they die from a lack of solidarity.

How many organised women are there in Honduras?

I can't give you an exact figure. All I can say is it's low. For example, there's an organisation of peasant farmers and agricultural workers and there are a few local organisations. And a women's movement is starting to get going inside the trade unions. Women in the trade unions take an active part in land occupations and campaigns for education, kindergartens, water and light. But these movements are headed by men.

Your committee calls itself Visitación Padilla, *women for peace. Who was this woman?*

Visitación Padilla is a kind of symbol for Honduran women. She was a teacher, writer and journalist. She was born in 1882 and lived until 1969. She had direct experience of North America's development as a capitalist power; she was against the interventionist policies of the US and was a committed anti-imperialist. She also fought against the military dictatorship of her time and against women's oppression. So her life was a microcosm of our own work and our vision of what peace means. All the elements we feel are necessary for freedom were united in her. Peace is the self-determination of people in a democracy, not just a formal democracy, but a democracy which works in solidarity with the disadvantaged and promotes equality between the sexes.

Footnotes
[1] The Esquipulas II Peace Accords were signed by all five Central American presidents in August 1987. They established a procedure for; an end to Contra aid, a ceasefire in countries beset with armed conflict, and a national dialogue within each country.

Olga Benoit and Marie Frantz Joachim (Haiti)

SOFA: A forum for rural women and market sellers

Over the past few decades Haiti's history has been dominated by the rule of the Duvalier family, with its violent repression, corruption and the impoverishment of the great majority of the population. The overthrow of Jean-Claude Duvalier (Baby Doc) in 1985 brought about few fundamental changes to the Duvalier social structure but it did open up a limited political breathing space. Despite repeated bloody attacks by the army and the *Tontons Macoutes*, Duvalier's death squads, Haitian popular organisations managed to expand this space. The climax of the widespread social and political mobilisation was the landslide victory of the left-wing priest, Jean Bertrand Aristide, in the presidential elections of December 1990.

Seven months later a military coup demolished the democratic experiment that had promised so much and Aristide was sent into exile. A new wave of repression began which has already claimed hundreds of victims among women activists in the social movements and has forced many to flee Haiti. International pressure, including a UN economic embargo, has so far failed to bring about Aristide's return. The economy, human rights and the environment continue to deteriorate.

This interview with Marie Franz Joachim and Olga Benoit from the women's organisation, *Solidarité Fanm Ayisyen* (SOFA), Haitian Women's Solidarity, took place before Aristide's election. But their opinions are still relevant if only because the brief democratic spring was unable to bring any lasting improvement in the situation of Haitian women who, incidentally, represent the bulk of the workforce. Women do 65 per cent of the work in the craft workshops and seventy per cent in light industry for wages of between two and three US dollars a day. Most of the female workers come from the countryside which is home to the majority of Haitian women. On average they have six to seven children and at least seventy per cent are illiterate.

* * * * * * * * * *

Could you say something about the development and importance of Haiti's feminist movement?

Marie Frantz: The feminist movement in Haiti has quite a long history. We choose 1934 as the starting point - the year when women set up the *Ligue Feminin d'Action Sociale* (Feminine Social Action League). As you might expect, most of the women who took part in this were from the bourgeoisie and petty bourgeoisie. They fought mainly for women's suffrage, just like women in Europe at that time. As it happens, smallholders, vendors and workers also supported the campaign for women's suffrage. After organising various demonstrations and other events, the league managed to found a girls' grammar school. They also secured access to university for women and eventually women's suffrage as well. Mind you, initially it was only for the election of magistrates, deputies and senators. Women weren't allowed to elect presidents until 1955.

During the fifties more and more women joined the workers' movement. In response to this, a women's coffee workers' union was founded and a union of female workers in the *Comme il faut* tobacco processing plant. After 1957 when Duvalier came to power, many women were active in both feminist and mixed political work simultaneously. A number of these women were persecuted and killed in horrendous prisons. As a result the movement disappeared. It was literally snuffed out by the dictator. But since Duvalier's fall in 1986, several new women's organisations have been founded. The mass mobilisation of 15,000 women on the streets of Port-au-Prince on 3 April 1986 is just one indication of this new phase.

Olga: The overthrow of Duvalier caused real euphoria and all the different sectors wanted to seize the moment to get organised. Of course the new women's groups didn't all have the same aims. You have to remember that everything happened in a very spontaneous, very improvised fashion at that time. Some people felt a desperate need to organise simply because they were finally able to join groups openly; they wanted to exchange ideas but had no actual programme. Many of these groups don't exist anymore, others pop up here and there once in a while, for example on 25 November (International Day Against Violence to Women), but then you might not ever hear from them again. This has got something to do with the difficult economic situation in Haiti.

What sort of women are organised today?

Olga: Generally it's women studying at the university, many of them in the female students' movement, but they don't put forward specific demands for women. The real women's organisations today are made up of peasants and women from the poor and working classes. Of course it's not a very powerful movement - just a series of women's organisations that exist side by side but they aren't united in a single movement. One reason why you only hear about the women's groups sporadically is that most of them don't even have their own meeting-place.

How many women are there in SOFA?

Marie Frantz: I can't give you exact figures but I can give you an outline of our structure. We're a national organisation that's divided into seven sectors: peasant women, working-class women, street vendors, housemaids and domestic servants, workers etc... SOFA peasant women are the most powerful - they have groups in seven of the nine *departements* of Haiti. On every level - whether it is regional, community, *departement* or national level - there are committees. So it's difficult to say exactly how many women are involved.

How does your organisation describe itself? As a feminist organisation or simply a women's organisation?

(...Laughter...) *Marie Frantz*: This term, 'feminism', it's a big problem for us and it's got all sorts of negative connotations. As a committed 'feminist', a woman can be treated like dirt. On the whole - obviously I can't speak for everyone in Haiti - the word 'feminism' seems to put the fear of death into people. Nevertheless, we do see ourselves as a feminist movement because feminism underpins the root of the problems we have to deal with at the moment. But when we use this word, we're accused of being lesbians, anticlerical etc. We're criticised for dividing the struggle and so on.

Where do these criticisms come from?

Olga: From both Right and Left. You know, in this country people don't like it when women organise and bring their problems to the table, and yet women's organisations linked to the Church like the street vendors' or women's groups are acceptable. But these groups don't deal with the whole truth because they don't ask any gender-specific questions.

Marie Frantz: They don't even talk about the specific form of verbal and physical violence women street vendors are subjected to. They're never asked whether psychological violence is done to them or whether they suffer daily violence at home. There's no space for that. As a feminist organisation, we've chosen a different path. We work to achieve women's liberation and to create a new self-awareness among women. Women who are not aware of their own problems are not in a position to change the world either.

How do men behave towards you? You said the largest group in SOFA are the women peasants. What do the husbands say when their wives become active in SOFA?

Olga: You know, the peasant groups are much more open than the other women's groups. For them the issue of whether they're 'feminine' or 'feminist' doesn't arise. They're much more concerned about how we relate to them and how we respond to their problems. But we don't tell them what their problems are, they identify them for themselves. We're only there to create a situation in which they can bring their problems to the table. At the end of the day they know themselves better than we do. So, anyway, we then look for a solution together. As far as men are concerned, we've got to work on our propaganda. When women are hounded by the authorities, the men get all geared up to protest about it. But women who've developed their own self-awareness can take their own action.

Having said that, in view of the privileges men enjoy in this country, it's not always easy for women to go to a meeting and just drop their work at home or in the fields. In fact, this causes endless problems. But we're still trying to make people sensitive to issues specific to women so that life becomes less grim for women in this country.

What is the key issue for Haitian women in the SOFA groups? Is there something that unites all women or does it depend on the sector?

Olga: One problem common to all the groups is *machismo*: men cannot bear the idea of women organising themselves. There's a whole propaganda machine against it. For example, SOFA is accused of being anti-clerical. A great many women in Haiti are very devout so it stands to reason that they wouldn't want to have any truck with an 'anti-clerical' institution. That kind of thing holds us back a great deal. There's heaps of slanderous propaganda like that around, especially in the countryside.

Marie Frantz: Women in SOFA are divided into groups according to their occupation so they concentrate on the specific problems arising from their respective areas of work. For example, in 1986 and 1987 the peasant women had a particular problem with a tax which was to be levied on the products they took to market. The women were already exploited enough as it was. Obviously this tax had repercussions which went far beyond the peasant groups because the price rises affected everyone who bought their products. In fact, everyone could have united against the tax. But it was the peasant women, as those most affected, who mobilised and got the tax abolished. Now there's another tax that's replaced the former one which is part of an IMF economic package adopted by the government. The end result is that the peasants have to pay an even higher tax than the one they got abolished just to be able to sell their products in the market. This tax is supposed to pay for repairs to the stalls and for cleaning, but of course the money finds its way into the pockets of... well...

Olga: It's always the way. You know what people in the government are like....

One question; why did the women peasants unite against the tax and not the men?

Marie Frantz: In Haiti the market is women's domain, whereas their husbands stay in the fields. The women are responsible for both: they work in the fields and they sell their products in the market.

So do women also hold the purse strings?

Marie Frantz: Yes, in theory. But there's so little money involved you can't really talk about economic power - especially if you think of all they have to do for the little they finally get out of it. It isn't even enough to feed the family properly. You see, there are no good roads in Haiti. The women have a hard time carrying their produce to market, some of it they have to carry on their heads. It's obvious that women in Haiti, particularly the peasants, play a big role in the economy of the country. But that doesn't mean they have much power. Basically, an expensive market, bad roads, plus a lack of hospitals and social services present problems for men as well as women. But it's worse for women.

It may seem like women don't complain about it much. But that's simply because of the institutionalised *machismo*. Society makes women think like this: 'My husband says x and y, so that's the way it is.' *Machismo* is supposed to be a cultural heritage accepted by women. That's not true. When women have the chance to speak, when there's space for that, then they say quite freely that *machismo* is a problem for them and they don't accept it. 'I'm forced to live with it,' they say. 'I just don't know how to talk about it at home.' You hear women saying that time and time again. You see, there's a lot of violence linked to *machismo* which is often even worse for women in the countryside.

Is there any protection for women in the Haitian legislature?

Marie Frantz: No, none at all. Not even for rape victims. In the past, it wasn't even part of the public consciousness that a woman could be raped. Today it's a bit different.

Olga: Men use rape to conquer women. Of course the women could go to the police afterwards. But they hardly ever do that because for a woman rape is a catastrophe in every respect. It's to do with the myth of virginity and the fear of not being accepted by any other man afterwards. So the woman stays with her rapist.

Abortion is against the law in Haiti as in all Latin American countries except Cuba. How do Haitian women cope with this problem?

Olga: In the only way they can which obviously has serious consequences. Many women die from unhygienic conditions and injuries. At the moment we're encouraging them to at least talk about their experiences. It'll be some time before we launch a campaign for the repeal of the law.

Surely part of the process is to give women information about contraception? What role do the multinational pharmaceutical companies play in this respect?

Olga: A massive one. Stacks of pills are on sale. Many of them can't be sold in other countries. Haitian women have already been made guinea pigs for a lot of pills. At the moment Minigynon, a product from Germany, is on the market. There are ads everywhere for it, on giant billboards and on the radio. We're very sceptical because this pill is much, much cheaper than other pills which are usually quite expensive. We really need more information about it from other women's groups abroad.

What is healthcare generally like in Haiti?

Olga: There's a serious lack of health services throughout the whole country : there are no hospitals, no clinics, nothing. And where centres do exist, there are no doctors, no nurses, no medical instruments. Even in Port-au-Prince there's no medical care for the poor or for those with low incomes. In the capital there's a state hospital which is supposed to be within people's means, but if you're admitted there for an emergency, there's nothing for you, no scalpels, no alcohol, no bandages, you have to buy everything. And that's getting worse by the day. Not to mention the situation in the countryside...

DEBATING THE SOCIAL MOVEMENT

Elizabeth Maier   (Mexico)

Sex and class as a single entity

Over the past few decades Mexico's political culture has been characterised by what is effectively a one-party dictatorship of the *Partido Revolucionario Institutional* (PRI), Institutional Revolutionary Party. Until 1988 the so-called opposition consisted of the right-wing conservative *Partido de Acción Nacional* (PAN), Party of National Action, a completely divided Left, and various 'opposition parties' which were mere off-shoots of the PRI and were founded to give the Mexican political system a democratic facade. Various factors have all kept the Mexican political system stable; social programmes designed to coopt political opponents, the promotion of a liberal climate coupled with targeted repression of radical opponents, and regular election rigging. At an international level, Mexico is perceived as a relatively democratic country.

In 1988 this lethargic political scene was briefly aroused by the presidential canditature of the PRI dissident, Cuauhtémoc Cárdenas, who stood as an independent. Supported by most left-wing groups and popular organisations, Cárdenas rapidly provoked the kind of democratic support not witnessed in Mexico for decades. Wholesale election rigging nevertheless secured the presidency for the official PRI candidate, Carlos Salinas de Gortari. But the fraud and deception surrounding the election caused mass protests throughout the country. It encouraged opposition forces to unite and prompted the creation of a large opposition party led by Cuauhtémoc Cárdenas, called the *Partido de la Revolución Democrática* (PRD), Revolutionary Democratic Party.

The surge of democratic organisation also prompted Mexican women's groups to create structures which would enable them to join in the debate about social democratisation. One of the most important results of this process was the founding of the *Benita Galeana* women's association, named after a famous leader of the Mexican women workers' movement. One of the co-founders of *Benita Galeana* is the sociologist and feminist scholar Elizabeth Maier, a North American by birth, who has been active in the Mexican women's and popular movements for twenty years. In the following interview she talks about the history and structure of this women's association.

* * * * * * * * * *

Why did you decide to set up the Benita Galeana association?

After the presidential elections in July 1988, a lot of people in Mexico were very angry about the election rigging because everyone was convinced that Cuauhtémoc Cárdenas should have won the election. A month later an announcement appeared in a daily newspaper inviting all women fighting for democracy to a meeting at the premises of the independent '19 September' seamstresses' trade union. Women from the political parties, feminists - in fact a whole variety of women - turned up. It was there we first discussed the idea of founding a women's association to address women's demands in the current political context. We discussed whether such a group should be linked to Cárdenas or be independent. Those of us who were in favour of an independent group won the day.

Which women's groups were in favour of an independent association?

A variety of groups and individuals; for example, the seamstresses, feminist groups, women from the PRT (Revolutionary Workers' Party), members of district organisations etc. The split was mainly between those who'd helped make Cárdenas' victory possible, but were far from being Cárdenas loyalists, and those who wanted to jump on the bandwagon and harness the women to Cárdenas' yoke.

How did the group get going and what areas of work are you now involved in?

Well, it took quite a long time to set up *Benita* from July to November 1988. We met once a week in the offices of various left-wing parties. Our first action was a press release in which we spoke out against the election rigging and made known our views on the political and economic issues of the day and on the handling of the country's crisis. At one of these meetings - it lasted a whole weekend - we finally decided on the name and three main principles which would determine our work: we were for democracy, against violence and for the protection of life. Shortly after that we drew up our manifesto in popular but 'feminist' language, presenting the whole situation from a woman's point of view and from our own standpoint. We didn't want to tag our demands onto the bottom of somebody's else's analysis.

You just said 'feminist language'. What is that? Is it a particular characteristic of people who work in Benita*?*

Well, one of our main aims is to make the links between gender and class. Each one of us can be categorised with reference to either of these but they're often treated quite separately, or rather, separate demands arise from each of them. We're keen to present both as a single entity and change our language accordingly.

But within the feminist movement, this union of gender and class is viewed sceptically, because for poor and working-class women the struggle to improve their living conditions always takes precedence, not their specific repression as women. How do you tackle this problem?

For us the two processes are interlinked.

What do you mean by that?

In the urban popular movement there are organisations like CONAMUP whose membership is ninety per cent women and who've had their own women's groups and organised regional women's meetings since 1981. I'd describe these meetings as feminist meetings but they don't use the word, feminism, because it tends to put people off here. The mass media encourage people to think that feminists are all lesbians, burn their bras, grab men and willingly have regular abortions. It's a very loaded term which is why those of us who work with the urban poor and working classes have decided not to use it. That's not to say we'd deny being feminists. We just think the demand for conditions which will enable people to survive takes priority.

Doesn't that prevent women from making gender-specific demands?

No, because gender-specific problems like violence, abuse, rape, and the right to sex education are dealt with in our workshops. And the idea of separating reproduction from pleasure is explored in the workshops too. In the days when there was no alliance between feminism and the popular movement, this point of view simply didn't exist.

One of your main concerns is the struggle for democracy. What does that mean to you?

We need to achieve democracy in all areas of life - relationships at home, for example, and within the social structure. We shouldn't just limit democracy to the elections or politics. We define democracy in relation to the repression we experience as women; in fact from the standpoint of all oppressed sectors of society. Having control over our lives is part of that too and the right to control our own bodies. But obviously democracy could mean something completely different to other groups like the indigenous women's group.

There are obviously diverging tendencies within the women's movement in Mexico as there are elsewhere. Here, a distinction is often made between authoritarian and democratic feminism. I take it you count yourself as belonging to the latter category?

In my opinion all the different groups have something authoritarian in them. I don't think there's anyone here who's completely democratic. All we can do is try to reach that point and *Benita* is one such attempt.

How would you define democratic behaviour?

For me it means not approaching a situation from a preconceived sectarian standpoint simply because you want to prevent the opposite view from triumphing, even when you've long lost sight of the real problem. I've taken part in discussions where I really couldn't work out what we were actually talking about any more. I think here in Mexico we're in the middle of a learning process; we're learning to deal with democracy and tolerance. Everything used to be so riddled with sectarianism that you never listened to other people's suggestions. You only thought of undermining them and making sure they lost the argument. I think democracy should include an ability to listen without bias, to take every opinion into account and create something new together.

You've been in existence now for one and a half years. How has the way you discuss things and the way you see yoursleves developed?

We respect one another and listen to each other. Our fundamental principle is that we make our decisions on the basis of consensus and not simply by voting. As a result, we've learnt to argue, to develop our powers of persuasion, and to lead discussions; you could describe it as an ideological struggle which for me has been an extremely interesting and exciting process.

Apart from yourselves, there are two other women's organisations; the

Red Contra la Violencia (*Network against Violence) and the* Coordinadora Feminista *(Feminist Co-ordinating Committee) which was only founded two months ago. What are the differences and similarities between the three organisations?*

The common aim is to change the position of women in society. The Network concentrates on one particular issue: violence against women. Apart from one party, the PRT, only NGOs are represented in it, which means that many of the women involved in the Network are also paid for their work. That makes it more efficient but also has a lot of potential for conflict. It means that many women from the mass organisations sometimes take the attitude: well, they should just go ahead and do it, after all they're getting paid for it. As for the *Coordinadora Feminista*, I went to their first meeting where it was obvious they mainly wanted to work on a woman's right to choose - in other words, the right to abortion. Although they do include the problem of violence against women in their work, in contrast to us and the Network, they look at it solely from the point of view of gender. They don't address the issue of class at all. In my opinion that's because they're mainly well-heeled, middle-class women.

So their starting point is that changes in a few paragraphs of the law will improve the situation for women in the popular movement?

Absolutely. Mind you, any legal reform passed in this area will not be attributed to the women's movement. President Salinas de Gortari will take all the glory. He's looking for popular support to square proposals on this with the Church.

Do you think Salinas will use the demands of the Coordinadora Feminista *for abortion to justify his policies?*

Yes, I think the decriminalisation of abortion is part of Salinas' programme for the Mexican population. His plan is to drastically check the population explosion which he's promised the World Health Organisation he'll do by the year 2000[1]. One of the current state campaigns recommends the twenty to thirty-five age range as the ideal time for reproduction. The basis for such a campaign is clearly the legalisation of abortion.

As an umbrella organisation, have you thought of trying to influence the policies of political parties and institutions? What will you do at the next elections?

Our main interest is grassroots work which involves making the women's and popular organisations as a whole more sensitive to women's issues. But beyond that, we also need to discuss the opportunities for nominating joint female candidates for the next election of deputies. If we decide to do that, we'll only consider working with the PRD or the PRT, definitely not with the PRI or the PAN.

But is it necessary to get involved at all?

Yes, we feel we should at least discuss it. I think it would be a mistake to use up all our energy on an election campaign. But if we do succeed in uniting both causes, it would certainly be an advantage to nominate female candidates who really represent the grassroots. In the process, we may get the chance to liaise more closely with other women's groups. Pooling membership lists between the *Coordinadora Feminista*, the *Mujeres en Lucha por la Democracia* (Women in the Fight for Democracy), the Network against Violence, the Association for Legislation Against Rape and ourselves would really make a lot of sense. An election alliance like that would certainly help us achieve demands specific to women. [2]

Postscript

Like all popular organisations *Benita Galeana* has been adversely affected by Salinas' capitalist modernisation policies. After three years the association lost members and hence the ability to mobilise. The involvement of organised women from the poor and working class sectors of society became more and more sporadic. *Benita Galeana* therefore had to make its aims more moderate. In 1991 its activities were essentially: publication of the *Mata Dando* magazine, support for female candidates in the election campaign, a forum for non-sexist education in July and a protest march on 25 November (Day Against Violence to Women). Elizabeth Maier is no longer involved in *Benita*.

Footnotes

[1] In December 1990 abortion was legalised in the state of Chiapas but after opposition from the Right it was made illegal again only a few weeks later.

[2] On 16 March, 1991, the National Women's Convention for Democracy was founded as a women's initiative for the municipal and parliamentary elections in August 1991 and became active in the way Elizabeth Maier wanted. See Claudia Colimoro's contribution in this book.

Carmen Alicia Echeverry, Nedier Gamba, Gladys Lagos (Colombia)

In support of steelworkers: a wives' or women's organisation?

Colombia's women's movement is very diverse: there are feminist groups which are mainly middle-class, traditional women's organisations with a humanitarian ethos and primarily supported by upper-class women, and countless women's groups in grassroots organisations which tend to describe themselves as 'feminine', rather than 'feminist'. Awareness of problems specific to women is increasing everywhere, as is networking between the different organisations. Meanwhile a growing number of women are rising to leadership positions in the trade unions and other mixed popular organisations.

The women of the *Asociación de Esposas de Trabajadores de SINTRASIDELPA Y SINTRAIME*, Association of Wives of Union Members of SINTRASIDELPA and SINTRAIME, first came together thirty years ago to support their husbands' struggles in the workplace. Today twenty women between the ages of 25 and 45 are active in the group. The formation of the *Asociación de Esposas* was prompted by survival. In other words, the men's jobs determine the standard of living for their whole families - reason enough for the wives to support their husbands' struggles.

Of the 542 employees of the Pacific Steelworks in Cali, the third largest town in Colombia, some 64 per cent are union members; 40 per cent in the trade union SINTRASIDELPA and 24 per cent in the metal industry trade union, SINTRAIME. Because of current neo-liberal economic policies, the metalworkers' jobs are now under threat, having been relatively stable in the past. The factories are due to be rationalised and wage costs reduced. Nevertheless the steelworkers still belong to the privileged seven per cent of employees in Colombia who can negotiate their pay increases and improve working conditions through collective bargaining.

Today the members of the Wives' Association consider themselves to be at a turning point: originally dependent on the men's trade union, they are now forging a degree of independence and are reflecting on their own development as a women's group.

* * * * * * * * * *

Could you tell me something about your experiences? Why was your group founded? And why did you unite as a steelworkers' 'wives' association'?

Gladys: The Wives' Association was founded to support the struggles of the workers and their trade unions, mainly during wage negotiations. It was founded thirty years ago but it's only in the last twelve years that it's been an on-going thing. My colleague, Carmen, who's also here, has been involved for all those twelve years.

Carmen: Hardly any of the founder members are involved anymore because the husbands of those wives have been pensioned off now.

Is there a wives' association for all the trade unions here or is it something unique to SINTRASIDELPA?

Gladys: Only a few trade unions have got wives' associations so, yes, it's quite unique. At a women's workshop we took part in recently there was a similar group to ours, a *Comité de Familiares de Trabajadores de Cemento del Valle*, Cement Workers' Families' Association.

Carmen: From what they were saying, their group is like a carbon copy of ours. Mind you, they're not a wives' association; they call themselves a families' association.

Was the wives' association founded at the same time as the trade union?

Gladys: A few months later. The lads in the union soon realised they'd need the help of their families.

So the original idea came from the men in the trade union, not from the women, is that right?

Gladys: No, it was the women's idea. They wanted to support the men, especially their husbands. There was also an association of workers' children but that doesn't exist anymore.

Was the workers' children's association also supposed to support the fathers?

Gladys: Yes, it was. There's one member left from this association, Nedier. She now works with us. She's actually the daughter rather than the wife of a steelworker. The other members of the Children's Association are all married now and are more detached from their families.

Carmen: Young people today don't like coming to meetings. They'd rather be out on the streets with their friends. The ones who used to be involved now have families of their own or else they're studying.

How do you support the men and the trade union?

Gladys: Oh, in lots of ways: let's see, we take part in the demonstrations organised by the CUT, the trade union confederation - we took our whole families on the Labour Day demo. We organise meetings when there's a labour dispute going on, especially in the factories. If there are negotiations going on we go to the factory with our children and our families and try to give the men a boost. Some of them are downright apathetic. We say to them: 'Look, you can't leave us on our own, come with us! Let's go to the office where the negotiations are going on. We've got to keep up the pressure! We're the ones who're affected!' Then they feel obliged to come with us. At first, they try and wheedle out of it. 'I haven't got the time, what would I do there?' they say. And we say: 'But, comrade, it's a problem for all of us! It's just not fair that a handful of us are having to fight for the rest of us. Let's go!' Well, then they haven't got a leg to stand on so they come with us. When we get there, we try and draw attention to ourselves and make a lot of noise to put the bosses under pressure. Sometimes we even occupy a radio station or something.

Carmen: Yes, we did that eight years ago at CALENO, a local Cali radio station. We marched right in and occupied the building. They were about to start shooting at us! They thought we wanted to attack them. Then we explained that we only wanted to defend workers' rights and that it was a peaceful occupation.

Gladys: During the negotiations two years ago we got together and organised a real stunt. When the workers went into the factory, we stormed the entrance and marched straight through onto the factory floor. My colleague here had rustled up some musical instruments and we 'played' in our own little orchestra. We made such a din! The people inside were ever so shocked. Then we made some more noise with a megaphone. That's our way of supporting the men.

Apart from SINTRASIDELPA, are there other trade unions in the factory?

Gladys: There are two. SINTRASIDELPA was an independent trade union up until two years ago but then two years ago a branch of a larger trade union federation was set up as well to cater for the current situation. These days you've got to be so well-organised because the state wants to get rid of the trade unions, lock, stock and barrel. So we have to look for new ways of organising like joining the national trade union federations.

Can the workers join both trade unions?

Gladys: Yes, the two unions made an agreement but the majority belong to SINTRASIDELPA.

Are there members of both unions in the wives' association or only of SINTRASIDELPA?

Gladys: Of both, the group's open to everyone. When there are courses or workshops on, we invite people from all over. Even women whose husbands aren't union members come along; they're still welcome. We see it as an opportunity to get the families involved and encourage the workers to join the union.

So you support the men, but what does the union do for you as women?

Carmen: On special days, on Mother's Day, for example, they organise parties for us. And at Christmas we all meet up and they give us presents if there's no strike on.

Gladys: Sometimes a comrade stands up and says, 'now the negotiations are over, we're inviting the Wives' Association to a meal!'

Nedier: But that only happens when someone suggests it. If no one says anything, then nothing happens!

Carmen: When we're invited on a course or something, then the men pay for our travel and expenses. That's quite important support for us.

Are all the members of your association housewives without paid work? Or do some earn an income?

Carmen: Most of us are housewives, only a few have paid work.
Gladys: We've got a lot of respect for our colleagues who've got jobs outside the home. They go to work, do the housework and still manage to spare a little time to work with the group. We really appreciate that.

Does your involvement in the association help you settle disputes at home?
Do you get more understaining from the men as a result?

Gladys: As far as family relationships are concerned, I'll give you an example of a married couple who came to our meeting yesterday. The husband joined the union fairly early on but behaved very badly when it came to his wife's membership of our association. The two of them had had a lot of rows for quite some time. They're quite old and their children are married. This change in their life, being alone, wasn't something they were coping with very well. To help her get over it, the wife came to the group which made her husband even madder. We talked to her about how best to handle the situation. It must've done some good because yesterday at the meeting her husband was very sympathetic and now seems to support his wife's participation.

Nedier: We organise lots of lectures and discussions about this type of problem. You see, the lads often don't understand what's causing these difficulties so we get psychologists to come and tell us about potential sources of conflicts in the family and how to change our home life. Things have often got better as a result. The women talk more to their husbands; they tell them about whatever's happened and have more things in common with them. This means they also get to hear from the men what's happened in the factory much sooner, what types of repression there are and so on. Bear in mind that the women often know very little about the working conditions in the factory. They don't always appreciate that the men have to work in very high temperatures with a high level of noise and suffer from considerable stress. In the past, the women were often very grumpy when the men came home: 'Why are you so late?', they'd snap. Well, this would often make the men so mad that they'd lose control and start slapping their wives. But now the women understand the men's work situation much better and are more willing to help the men.

Yes, I can see that. But your work seems to be very heavily concentrated on the men. Surely women also have a lot of problems at home. Women are usually expected to be understanding towards their men. But men don't make nearly as much effort to understand us. Does the association also try to get the men to understand the women a bit better?

Gladys: Yes we do. We've recognised that we have to make the men more sensitive so that men also make an effort with us and share our workload. Quite often when a colleague is invited to a meeting, the problem arises as to who's going to look after the children or make the meal. Clearly, the man should step in to help. Some of the husbands of the women who came to our meeting yesterday stayed at home to look after the kids. Yes, we do realise that it's important to look at the whole family's problems, not just the worker's.

The steelworkers' union was very deeply affected by political repression. During the wave of arrests in 1990 many members were arrested. What did you do in this situation? How did you react?

Gladys: Our trade union was the most affected. When someone was arrested, we usually got to hear about it pretty quickly. The wife of a colleague who was in the union executive and a very committed member of our Association let us know at once when somebody's house had been searched or one of our comrades had been arrested. We'd then go straight to the trade union headquarters to discuss what to do. Normally we'd drive as fast as we could to the barracks where most of the detainees were taken. We then took turns standing guard at the entrance to stop them smuggling out the prisoners without anyone noticing. That's how they make them 'disappear', if you get what I mean. We all took part in this action - men *and* women.

Carmen: Our men were also imprisoned by the security police, the DAS. We kept a constant watch there as well. I truly believe that because of our actions, they couldn't make the men 'disappear'. At that time a good few people were arrested and then disappeared, you know. The way they arrested them and the things they said to them implied they wanted to make most of them disappear.

Gladys: But we do have one victim to mourn: our colleague, Ana Silvia Gómez, the wife of a trade union leader. She contracted cancer of the pancreas because of the repression and the stress it caused her. She died very quickly, after only three months of getting ill.

I gather she's the women in whose memory you're going to organise an event.

Gladys: Yes, that's right. She was a very dear friend and colleague. A great fighter. She had a big heart for anyone who'd suffered injustice. She empathised with people as though it'd happened to her personally.

What was the background to this wave of repression? There weren't any wage settlements. Often repression increased during labour disputes, doesn't it?

Gladys: Well, the collective bargaining went on between October and December 1989. On 1 March 1990 the arrests began. I suppose the wave of repression had something to do with the previous negotiations. Of course the state cites other reasons: guerrillas, subversion, that sort of thing. A colleague of ours still has to keep going to court - he's charged with having something to do with a kidnapping. Because of these kind of accusations, two of our friends had to give up everything and leave the country, taking their families with them.

During your protests were you also harassed by the military? Or are the military more considerate when it comes to women?

Carmen: No, not at all. The military gave us a really hard time! But we didn't give up. We knew something serious could happen to us but we didn't let it divide us. Unity is strength! If any one of us had had to stand alone, something could easily have happened to her. They could have arrested her and made her disappear. So we always stuck together. Maybe that's why nothing happened to us in front of the barracks.

Gladys: It's a critical situation because they're always trying to provoke you. So we women always have to be on the lookout for people who might be following us. When we walked or drove anywhere we always saw suspicious cars and motor bikes tailing us.

Carmen: Obviously you feel very frightened but you don't let them see it.

Gladys: Here in Cali it's often thought that women are too scared to go into the prisons because the searches are so terrible. It acts as a deterrent. But when our men were finally sent to Villahermosa prison after being shoved about by the police station, the DAS and the barracks, we were off in a flash to visit them. It was very important for us to see them and show them our solidarity.

Carmen: Even women who aren't members of our association came with us to the prison.

Are there very strict examinations for prison visits? Vaginal examinations?

Gladys: Yes, it's all very unpleasant.

Do you have much contact with other women's groups, trade unions or human rights groups? Or do you tend to keep yourselves to yourselves?

Nedier: No, we're a very open group. We exchange experiences with other trade unions, with colleagues from the Nestlé trade union in Bugalagrande. We've also tried to organise the women from Quintex, a textile factory, and colleagues from other factories. We meet frequently with women from the university. No, it's fun to share our experiences with other people. After all, they're wonderful experiences!

I still don't quite understand: Do you see yourselves more as a wives' or as a women's association? Your work is concentrated more on supporting your husbands and not so much on improving your situation as women.

Nedier: I've been doing this work for a long time now and for as long as I can remember the men have been in charge. They've arranged things like tailoring courses for us or courses to learn how to sew trousers. Everything's been arranged through their support. Once we were approached by a group which did consciousness-raising work and it turned into a right old argument. The union said: 'No, the women are there to support *us*!' As if we were their crutches! But now we've reached a turning point. We're starting to value and appreciate ourselves more and we don't want to be the men's crutches anymore!

Gladys: Basically, I think we've become independent. In the past, our big meetings were always organised by the men. Not this time. We've arranged the day and the programme. Obviously we have to bear in mind that collective bargaining is coming up again soon and because of the labour reform the negotiation phases have now been shortened to a month. So we've put wage settlements on the programme. But we also want to look at women's identity. We want to be there for the women at this time when we're trying to strengthen our identity and autonomy. For many women it's a sensitive subject. If you invite them to a lecture or workshop about it, they don't come. But they come to a tailoring course, no problem.

Nedier: When you say: 'come to the meeting and bring saucepans and lids with you', they're happy to oblige and they bring the whole family along to make a good racket. Sure, when there are big labour disputes, women enjoy taking part in the demonstrations and shouting slogans. But they don't like the lectures. So it's often difficult to find a way of changing their outlook. But lots of them have already changed. They understand it's important to organise discussions or meetings or demonstrations. Now it's also become important for them to talk to each other and reflect on who they are and why they're doing certain things. It's still the case that if you ask a woman at a demo, 'why are you shouting? Why are you doing that?' she's likely to say, 'the men in the union have said we should shout and fight.' But that's starting to change now. These days, when you ask a woman, 'why are you doing all that, why are you fighting?' she'd probably say, 'to get more guarantees of work and more stability, or things like that.' The women have many more criteria of their own these days.

What activities are there? How frequently do you meet?

Gladys: We meet every fortnight, always on a Saturday because of the women who go to work. Saturday is also a good day, because the kids can look after the house then. That's important, considering how little security we have and the risk of burglary.

Do you meet here at the trade union offices?

Nedier: Yes, but at the moment we're trying to decentralise things by meeting at a colleague's house or in a park, outdoors where it's green. Here in this building it gets unbearably hot at three or four in the afternoon.

How do you organise your work?

Gladys: We sort out a work programme. Everyone's involved in making suggestions for the programme. Sometimes there are lectures which the kids come to as well. In the last two years we've had lots to do on the new constitution and the labour reform. We often show videos. We've got lots of other ideas too. For example, one woman has suggested organising a kindergarten. And we want to open a sort of co-operative shop.

How far have you got with this shop?

Nedier: Well, there have been stumbling blocks! Some of the men supported us, others didn't think we were up to it. They're so pessimistic. They see a problem in everything and predict failure before we've even begun. They asked us where we were going to get the money. We said we were counting on their support. Finally a colleague of ours cooked up the idea of including the proposal for the co-operative shop as an item in the coming wage negotiations. It's the first time the men have introduced an item of ours onto the list of demands! We hope we can get an interest-free loan because we need 1.5 million pesos as initial capital. We've already started collecting money with raffles, bazaars, bingo and things like that.

How do you intend to organise the shop?

Carmen: Everyone would pitch in - some with the management and some at the till. Everyone can help wrap things up. We're planning to buy the goods wholesale in sacks, and then sell them in kilo packets. We're going to work by the hour and take turns. It'll all be voluntary work, at least to start off with.

Gladys: We're going to invest our time for free at first because it won't work if we have to pay wages. We have to sell the goods cheaply; it's a community project, so the profits will be very low.

Nedier: The problem is, there are very few of us now. If the two of us don't come, then there's no one to carry on. But us two aren't the leaders, we're not in charge. We don't manage everything. The other women are very on the ball. They often get things together themselves.

Gladys: Yes, but I suppose we do have to motivate them.

Nedier: Yes, and what the men say to them often has a demoralising effect. They just need to ignore it, put their noses to the grindstone and get on with the job.

Gladys: About three years ago the association fell into a bit of a rut. A colleague of ours fancied herself as a leader but she didn't know how to relate to the women. She was very demanding and really didn't get on with anyone.

How did you come to be in charge of the association's work?

Gladys: Probably because we've stuck at it all these years. I certainly never intended to take control. I've only ever wanted to improve myself. But I think we took over the work here because we enjoy it. I like being active.

What do your husbands think of your work? Men often get upset when women become active. Maybe they think a bit of activism is a good thing, but more than a bit is too much for them!

Gladys: I'm here because my husband helps at home. They told him about the Assocation at the union. He told me about it and I liked the idea. I've been involved for eleven years now. At first it was all quite badly organised. Lots of women came just to talk about their husbands:

'he didn't come home last night. Just where was he...' There were lots of fights. You simply met for the sake of meeting, without any particular reason. I stopped coming as a result. But when my husband became a member of the union executive, he mentioned one day that the Association was going to fold. The new union executive finally organised a meeting about it and I suppose the new group started from there.

You don't have an elected or appointed coordinating committee, so is it just the ones who do the most work who end up coordinating things?

Gladys: Yes. We can only afford a secretary and two treasurers on our meagre savings. We haven't appointed a chairwoman or deputy chairwoman because that way there are no differences between us and we're all equal. We have a facilitator at our meetings, that's all. Otherwise there'd be no discipline.

How many of you are there?

Gladys: Sometimes twenty come to the meetings, sometimes eight.

Nedier: The women come when you call them. You really have to work at it - go up to them, explain everything to them. When there are negotiations - like at the moment - then 23 come.

Have these 23 been members for a long time or do they only participate in your activities from time to time?

Gladys: That depends. Some only stay a short while and then disappear again, others work with us continuously. Of course the group was much stronger eight years ago. There were about eighty women then. That was the time they occupied the factory and the radio station.

Nedier: That was a very special time. I was involved in so many activities. Really old women came then, the wives of retired workers. They got into fights with the watchmen, even with the factory bosses. When there was a strike on they didn't let a single worker into the factory. It was all-out war.

Gladys: Today it's different. Two years ago we still stormed the gates and held a meeting on the factory site. But after the arrests last year many people have become more timid. Some of the women whose husbands were arrested have stopped coming to the meetings altogether.

Nedier: Quite a few of the women we've visited at home recently have said: 'I'm afraid to go to the union, perhaps they'll make my husband disappear.'

Gladys: You just have to mention the union and people get scared. You see, the state has given the unions a guerrilla image; people really look at you suspiciously!

Nedier: You can't even demand higher wages. If anyone does, they think: 'ah, a union member!' And bang, he's dead. Here a human life doesn't even cost 10,000 pesos. You can be murdered for just 5,000 pesos.[1]

Gladys: The fact that the state describes union members as guerrillas has serious consequences. When my husband was elected to the union executive, my little daughter and my son said: 'Daddy, are you a guerrilla?' So you can see how effective this propaganda is!

Nedier: That's why there's so much apathy here.

How do the men in the union respond to your work?

Nedier: They admire the way we organise ourselves; we sense that quite frequently. Normally wives simply don't organise, just men. In general, the men are very proud to be supported by the women, even though they sometimes don't support us!

Gladys: At least my husband supports me when I have to leave the house. At the moment I reckon he'll be cooking supper.

Nedier: My husband doesn't support me - I don't have one! But I do have my parents at home. My father's very proud of me when I get involved and protest, take action! He likes it a lot. My mother's quite the opposite. At first she was afraid something might happen to me, that I'd be arrested or something. She doesn't understand. An older sister of mine behaves exactly the same as her.

Does your father work at the steelworks?

Nedier: Yes, he's been there for 27 years. He's a member of SINTRAIME, the metalworkers' industrial trade union.

So your mother never joined the association?

Nedier: Never. She's a very traditional woman. The house must always be clean, the meal must always be ready when Dad and the kids come home. She couldn't bear it if Dad didn't get his juice served to him when he comes from work. I've tried to take her with me to the group. 'Just leave the stress behind at home for once, enjoy yourself a bit,' I say to her. But she doesn't want to come.

Have you got any sisters?

Nedier: Yes, four. But I'm the only one to turn out like my father. My sisters are very domestic, they hardly ever go anywhere. But I feel good working with groups, travelling around, doing things!

Footnotes

[1] One US dollar is approximately 500 pesos (1991)

Maritza Villavicencio (Peru)

The feminist movement and the social movement: willing partners?

The women's movement and the feminist movement are not synonymous terms either in Europe or in Latin America, even if they are often treated as such. The women's movement is the more comprehensive term, incorporating all women who organise autonomously around mutual interests. The feminist movement includes all women who organise to fight for the rights and emancipation of women and against the patriarchal structure of society. The relationship between the women's movement and the feminist movement is one of tension. Feminists often criticise women's groups in the social movements or trade unions for only fighting for short-term demands and not questioning the patriarchal structure of society. For their part, the women in the social movements reject the feminists' attempts to claim ideological leadership of the women's movement.

The historian, Maritza Villavicencio, is dismissive of such polarisations. In the following article she describes the heterogeneous origins and development of the two different forms of feminine political activism with reference to the history of the Peruvian women's movement. She calls for recognition of the fact that in different phases of development different sectors are the driving force of the movement and should thus take over the ideological leadership accordingly. She wants her article to be expressly understood as the perspective of a woman who has considered herself part of the feminist movement since its inception.

* * * * * * * * * *

The History of Peruvian Feminism

The Peruvian feminist movement was created in 1978 by middle-class women: academics, students and intellectuals. In recent years a handful of women from the urban poor and working classes have joined them, but in the absence of a mass membership, the basic social composition remains unchanged. The urban middle-class identity of Peruvian feminists has left an indelible mark on their political behaviour. The middle classes tend to see the state as the main agent of social change. This has led to strategies designed to rebuild the nation and democratise Peruvian society through strong state leadership. It means that the focus of their activity is the state apparatus which they themselves have helped to create. They see change as starting from the top and working down. During Velasco Alvarado's government, 1968-75, middle-class women played an active role in the democratisation of the state - a role which went beyond their class identity. But they never gained any leadership positions nor did they get involved in the process on behalf of their own sex. With few exceptions, they were excluded from the corridors of power.

The feminists were part of a radical generation of leftwing students. There was a time when the lecture theatres were teeming with Marxists, socialists and communists and it is here that nearly all the parties of the New Left were born. The female students were swept along in this political whirlwind. While they did not consciously raise gender-specific demands, they were aware of the opportunities which political activism gave them for defeating sexism. Years later they realised this was a delusion. The left-wing parties simply reproduced the age-old gender-specific division of labour and power, thus hindering women's advance.

The first feminist groups came from the ranks of these dissatisfied women. Since there was no role for them in the left parties, feminists from the modern urban districts of Lima modelled themselves on cosmopolitan middle-class women in Europe and North America and treated them as a yardstick for their own identity. They imitated the fashions, gestures and appearance of feminists from those countries and became active, employed, intellectual, modern women who determined their own sexuality, had fewer children, or better still, were neither mothers nor housewives and wore the Indian clothes fashionable at that time. In other words, their cultural identity was elitist: it bore no relation to the everyday life of the majority of Peruvian women or even the everyday life of women in Lima.

The influence of this metropolitan femininism has also seeped into the ideological sphere. Peruvian feminism has been coloured by a debate in Europe and North America in the early 1970s which is often described as the second phase of international feminism. From this phase comes the guiding principle: 'the personal is political', which dominated the big demonstrations and struggles for civil rights, for the legalisation of abortion, against sexual violence and for voluntary motherhood. Feminists in Peru instantly donned this political slogan. In fact, their political alignment was identical to that of international feminism right from the start. It is this ideological framework which has created a gap between the feminists and the reality of Peruvian women, as well as the grassroots social movements who represent them.

But we feminists developed differently from those whom we appeared to imitate in one decisive aspect: European and North American feminists embraced 'the personal is political' principle only after they had moved through the following stages. First they started to complain about having to do all the housework on their own. Then they began to realise that this was the reason why they were unequal to men in the race to get on in the system. In this way the revolt began at home; from the fight over who looked after the children to arguments about sharing the housework. It soon became apparent that there was no solution to these conflicts in the private domain so the women took their personal problems out into the open. They began with small consciousness-raising groups discussing things like group dynamics and ended up on mass demonstrations in the thick of a major political debate. This debate achieved legitimacy because the women were expressing their real, practical, everyday experiences.

In short, the feminist movement became a strong social movement which was given a political coating by its protagonists and thus managed to put the entire social and political system under pressure.

By contrast, the roots of Peruvian feminism do not lie in the general dissatisfaction of women as a whole or of the women of a particular social class. It was founded by a clearly circumscribed group of women, namely the academics, students and intellectuals in the capital, who have political experience behind them and are seeking a leading role in the political arena. They are sick of being second-class citizens and second-class political activists. They are fighting for equal rights and opportunities so that they can determine the political life of the country on a par with men. That is the main motive for their political activism.

As a result, Peruvian feminism is a *political* women's movement in contrast to the socially-orientated women's movements to be found in urban popular organisations, professional organisations, trade unions and regional associations. Ironically, Peruvian feminists define themselves in their writings and lectures as a social movement, albeit a social movement without a mass following. But they use abstract, theoretical arguments to support these claims without reference to their actual development or the general political context or their relationship to other social and political activists.

The Different Tendencies within The Women's Movement

When considering the relationship of the feminist movement to the *social* women's movement, we must first define the term, 'women's movement.' In Peru today there are various forms of social and political expression by women but my analysis is limited to *urban* movements for two reasons: firstly, this is where the hub of the feminist movement lies and, secondly, the main impulses for change over the last few decades have come from social groups in the towns. Moreover it is in the urban sector that the most recent phenomenon in the women's movement has appeared - namely the new groups developing economic survival strategies.

In fact the urban poor and working-class women's organisations are among the most active sectors of the women's movement. They include women's organisations running communal soup kitchens and survival stop gaps, and trade unions. The 'political' factions of the movement consist of women who are either active in a political party or those who are independently politically active. I am more concerned with the left of the political spectrum since it is the stamping ground for the feminist organisations. There is also the feminist faction, which I've already mentioned, consisting of small groups of politically active women who work on different issues like reproductive rights, communication and violence against women. This faction includes independent women, feminist centres or institutions and organisations. In recent years a new alliance has been formed between the political and feminist factions which, in turn, has established links with women in the grassroots social movement. The alliance consists of social workers and community workers working with women's organisations in the poor and working-class sectors.

The Relationship of the Feminist Movement to Social Women's Movements
First Phase: 1978-1982

In their own analyses feminists describe this phase as a time of confusion and indifference on the part of left political parties and the social movement. Activity focused on support of trade union struggles which used up a lot of energy and relegated the conflict with patriarchal power to the back-burner. These analyses stress the negative side of the first phase, particularly the alleged self-sacrifice of women.

Towards the end of the seventies large-scale social and political upheavals were instigated by the popular movement and the trade union movement. The trade unions had an indisputable hegemony over the entire movement and in effect all forms of social expression were brought about or led by them. Inevitably, feminism, which was only just developing at that time, got caught up in these struggles. Gender-specific perspectives were frantically developed in a wide range of contexts. This was also a time of associations and alliances which culminated in various forms of joint action.

So in this first phase, the women's committees in the political parties (either newly formed or reactivated), plus the first women's organisations in the urban poor and working classes and the first feminist organisations co-existed with equal rights. Each developed independently and none was prepared to accept the political line or hegemony of another. To be frank, few were even in a position to take a leading role in the women's movement. The absence of leadership in the women's movement affected the feminists particularly strongly. It was the determining factor in the transition to a second phase.

Second Phase: 1982-1983

During this period the movement went into retreat. It chose to separate itself from the other tendencies and the search for an identity began. With hindsight this phase seems like a time of preparation for the return to the public eye and institutionalisation because all feminist activities later took place within the framework of new institutions. A series of non-governmental institutions were created from which the feminists directed themselves towards society and towards the other tendencies. And so it was that they entered the third phase in a much more powerful position. In 1983 the Second Feminist Meeting of Latin America and the Caribbean took place in Lima, exerting a major influence on the movement.

Third Phase: 1984-1986

The feminists were now intent on making their voice heard in the public political arena. In this respect, they considered themselves to be at the vanguard of the women's movements and felt confident about representing the political ideology of all women. But the other movements had also moved on. The political movements which had previously been active had fallen by the wayside; meanwhile the urban poor and working-class sectors had undergone a significant transformation. By this time the women active in the soup kitchens and the glass-of-milk committees[1] had organised big demonstrations as independent organisations. They had achieved significant changes, not only in the urban poor and working-class sectors, but also within the popular movement. They were challenging traditional political strategies from a gender-specific standpoint and as marginalised sectors trying to bring about liberation from the bottom up. Even sociologists began to take an interest in these new social movements.

By contrast, the feminists continued to pursue their 'from the top down' approach and tended to devalue the achievements and opinions of the women's organisations in the poor and working-class sectors. By criticising the lack of political alignment in these organisations, they were indirectly presuming the need for a vanguard to provide such an orientation. Naturally the feminists envisaged that they would act as the vanguard.

Perhaps we should take a closer look at the feminists' criticisms of the working-class women's organisations. One assertion was that the soup kitchens reinforced women's bondage to housework. This appears to be neither verified nor refuted by existing studies. The actual statements of the women themselves, who stress the political aspect of their work and their own personal development, seem more essential to me, for they succeeded in creating space and time for themselves through their work in the soup kitchens.

Another criticism was that the state and public administration were relieved of the burden of their social responsibility by these organisations. This criticism has often directed at charitable organisations providing food aid. From time immemorial, the failure of the Peruvian state to fulfuil its social responsibility towards the population has been a characteristic of the ruling classes in whose hands state power has rested. A glance at the situation in the slums, euphemistically called 'new villages', or the women's organisations there, would only serve to confirm this. But if we consider the political and historical development of the relationship between the state and the inhabitants of the poor neighbourhoods, then it becomes clear that their relationship has changed.

The political parties, the feminists, the NGOs and the politically active intellectuals had no concrete, acceptable and practical alternatives to things like soup kitchens which were set up without the assistance of any aid programmes, from the women's firsthand experience of struggle. Their aim was to combat the exploitation and manipulation by the state and by international charitable organisations which women from the poor neighbourhoods are subjected to. The participation of the so-called *pobladoras*, the slum dwellers, in the teachers' strikes in the late 1970s provided the impetus for creating the 'soup kitchens'. At the same time, a progressive arm of the Catholic church was looking for an opportunity to reorganize its work with the women in the poor neighbourhoods and wanted to get away from traditional forms of assistance. An important factor in the organisation of the soup kitchens was naturally the attitude of the women themselves who considered the work they had to do in return for food aid from official organisations, for example from government agencies, to be damaging to their health.

But as if that were not sufficient, these women's organisations also had a great capacity to mobilise people which they developed independently of the feminist movement and the political parties. They did not stop at demanding public services (running water, transport, etc) nor did they merely seek solutions to their survival problems. They also had to fight for the preservation and independence of their own organisations.

There is no cooperation between independent women's organisations and organisations promoted by the state because the latter were founded and conceived with the intention of destroying independent forms of organisation. To a certain extent the women have defended and protected their structures on their own. They have developed tactics and strategies ranging from negotiation to confrontation. The glass-of-milk committees, for example, managed to defend the independence of their organisation against takeover bids by the APRA-led[2] municipal government by organising street blockades and a march to the presidential palace. Nevertheless the government's promotion of 'client' organisations and its manipulative tactics will continue to pose a real danger.

A further criticism is that hierarchical structures remain untouched in the poor neighbourhoods and women are rarely appointed to permanent leadership positions. In fact this point is very complex and central to the understanding of the position of the feminist movement towards these organisations. From 1985 onwards, in feminist analyses of these so-called functional organisations, the importance they attach to the personal development of their members was stressed. It is widely accepted that these organisations support the development of a personal sense of identity and have a progressive effect on the family, the private domain.

But apart from this positive evaluation, the impact of these organisations on the public and political sphere has either been insufficiently analysed or completely ignored. And yet it is precisely the relationship of their struggle to the public sphere that is criticized the most heavily. Their independence, which the women defend, is challenged and described as 'an inclination towards self-marginalisation' or as fear of direct confrontation with male power.

The feminists (like most people) are ignorant of the political impact of the local women's organisations. Either that or they don't want to acknowledge it because they themselves have opted for a different political strategy. The feminists strive to share power within existing institutions and patriarchal power structures. In 1985, for example, the feminist movement participated in the parliamentary elections, supporting two candidates on the list of the *Izquierda Unida* (IU), United Left, but they did so without launching any sort of anti-patriarchal struggle within the IU. Even criticism of IU party structures and of the Left in general was quietly avoided.

To sum up, we are talking about two different perspectives. First of all, the feminists want access to the arenas of power and decision-making currently dominated by the patriarchy. Once they have achieved this, they will develop programmes in favour of women as a whole. To that extent they behave or present themselves as representatives of the entire sex, whereas women from the poor and working-class sectors have taken the opposite route. Starting from their collective, organised experience of the grassroots, they aim to change their political and social surroundings. As a result of their daily confrontations, the existing power structures are fundamentally challenged. Consequently, the prospect of increased power for women in the *prevailing* power structures is of minimal interest to many women leaders, which is why they don't feel represented by the feminist movement.

The final criticism, perhaps the most important for the feminist movement, is that women from the popular organisations have not managed to make gender-specific demands, or if they have, they are only vaguely formulated and are either watered down or completely lost within the general demands of the poor and working-class sectors. It should be emphasised here that it was the feminist movement in Peru which first introduced the concept of gender-specific problems. But even if that is to their credit, in their efforts to preserve this concept, they have ignored all the 'general' problems which may also affect women.

In this sense the feminist movement always stands in opposition to other movements and even to other forms of the women's movement. For example, in political work, the feminists draw a dividing line between the issues of 'general politics' and 'our issues', between 'our gender-specific demands' and 'general demands', 'our forces' and 'those of the others'. This position, promoted by Peruvian feminism since 1984, was lucidly profiled in 1986 in Maxine Molyneux's[3] theoretical study of the participation of women in the Nicaraguan revolution. Molyneux claims that women's interests can be divided into three categories, of which two are gender-specific. In her view, practical gender-specific interests are those which arise from women's position in the gender-specific division of labour and those related to her reproductive duties: the well-being of the family, the children etc... These goals are short-term. According to

Molyneux there are also economic or financial demands related to survival. They are made in the private, family domain and its immediate surroundings within the poor and working-class sectors.

These demands in themselves do not lead to any real emancipation so other strategic, gender-specific ones have to be added: demands aimed at destroying the roots of women's subordination, challenging and changing the gender-specific distribution of labour, fighting for the independence of women as people in their own right, destroying the institutionalised oppression of women... These are long-term goals and their demands are historical because the demand for personal liberation postulates liberation for all. These demands belong in the political sphere of the feminist movement, according to Molyneux. This interpretation rests on the basic premise that the actions of women in the poor and working-class sectors can only lead to a fragmentary and partial awareness of their subordinate position, whereas feminists, on the other hand, have total vision and a 'comprehensive awareness of women's subordination'.

Despite the danger of strategic interests remaining in the abstract, the way forward is for feminists to 'bring awareness' to the women in the poor and working-class sectors. But let's take a closer look at women from the poor and working-class sector in their own surroundings. From the moment a woman and her family occupy a piece of land and through sheer perseverance begin to make it habitable, individual and private, family domains are mingled with collective, public and communal ones. The roles of woman, mother and *pobladora* all overlap. There are no clear distinctions between the private and the public and no restriction of a woman's social and physical reproductive duties to a particular domain. Women internalise the complexity and diversity of their practical work and so the awareness that arises out of it cannot be one-sided. The demands women evolve and the manner in which they become involved in these will be equally as fluid as their practical work. That explains why these women defend their own families' right to well-being just as enthusiastically as the independence of their organisation and their own leadership role within this organisation.

In this sense the many-sided strategy of the new women's organisations within the urban poor and working-class sectors makes an extraordinarily valuable contribution to an alternative strategy for social and political change: it comes from the combined interest in accumulating power collectively and in responding practically to their pressing needs. It has resulted in an active cooperation between organisations which tend to be grassroots-oriented and more broadly based co-ordinating committees, associations and assemblies.

Fourth Phase: 1986 to the present

This phase began around the second half of 1986 when the poor and working-class women's organisations were engaged in a major struggle on several fronts - the town councils, their communities and the party structures - against takeover bids by government programmes of the then-APRA government and by the left parties. In order to resist these takeover bids, the organisations decided to re-structure and consolidate their independence. As a result of this process, the first steps were taken towards creating a political programme. Events such as the First National Meeting of the Soup Kitchens in June 1986 and the First Assembly of the Glass-of-Milk Committees in Lima in October 1986 clearly illustrated that such a programme could be achieved by centralising and combining forces and experience.

Keen to promote democracy for the poor and working-class sectors, participants in these meetings emphasised their right to speak and to participate in all major arbitration processes affecting them. In this way the women achieved the right to be represented in the regional assemblies for the preparation of the National People's Assembly (ANP). They also took part in the First National Feminist Meeting (September 1987).

Just as women in the popular movement challenged and partially changed all the different areas they became involved in, so they also influenced the feminist domain, though at first they raised their specific problems rather indirectly. Their direct participation was encouraged by a feminist group formed at the end of 1986.

It took a long time for Peruvian feminists, like Latin American feminists in general, to discuss the connection between class and gender-specific problems on a theoretical, ideological level, let alone to introduce it into their practical programmes of work. In my opinion, the reassessment of the feminist perspective can be traced back to a mutual *rapprochement* at that time between specific groups of feminists and women from the poor and working-class sector. Their new position was first articulated in early 1987 by Rocio Palomino[4] who proposed that the movement should open itself up to other social sectors and that activities described as 'feminist' should be more accurately defined. The proposal was aptly presented at the First National Feminist Meeting (1987), in which women from the popular organisations from Lima and the provinces took part.

This was the crux of the matter for the feminists: either the demands and the reality of the majority of women in Peru had to be taken into account and integrated into feminist progammes or a division was likely to occur, where only quite specific points from the popular movement would be taken up, without fundamentally changing the prevailing debate or our political mode of operation.

But there are other factors which will also affect the future of Peruvian feminists: the economic crisis and terrorism.[5] The economic crisis has prompted the majority of workers and smallholders, male and female alike, to defend their right to a basic standard of living. Instead of demanding an improvement in the quality of life, it's now a question of defending life itself. Hunger, terrorism and state repression are omnipresent. Women's organisations fighting for survival are the most active these days. It is they, in contrast to other social and political activists, who have taken the greatest political initiative and are still able to mobilise and motivate others.

We feminists must take this reality into account in creating our strategy for building a broadbased, comprehensive women's movement. That does not mean that women from the poor and working-class sectors and those in survival organisations will always be the driving force behind society and the movement. They happen to be such a force in this phase, just as the feminists were in their time. It is important to be flexible enough to acknowledge this. No one in the women's movement can lay claim to a hegemony without time limits.

For the women's movement today, terrorism and state repression are the second most important issue after the economic crisis. Women are primarily affected as the mothers, wives and daughters of those who have been disappeared, tortured or executed but they are also the victims of violence themselves, whether as part of a terrorist's family or as part of the machinery of repression. This situation is likely to get worse: the paramilitary organisations are not only doubling their efforts to recruit women but are also trying to infiltrate the leadership of the women's movement.

It is conceivable that the women's survival organisations could become a protective wall for the entire movement for several different reasons: firstly, in their short history they have accumulated a lot of experience in defending and protecting their own indepedence. Secondly, they have concrete aims and ideas as opposed to the political parties' abstract programmes which only allow women secondary roles. Thirdly, their organisation has not been attacked until now and is still respected by the paramilitary groups because their roots lie in the poor and working-class sector.[6] Fourthly, they give women's reproductive role a new dimension: the preservation of life stands in opposition to the terrorist discourse of violence and power. And fifthly, they present one of the few practical ways out of the crisis - ways which have come from the grassroots and at least give our society a ray of hope.

Footnotes

[1] Glass-of-milk, (*Vaso de Leche*), programme was initiated by the United Left (IU) municipal government in 1983, and guaranteed by law in 1984 to distribute milk amongst needy children in Lima. *Vaso de Leche* is run by cooperative community networks in which each mother particpates once a week.

[2] APRA - a party with a social democratic orientation, which formed the government from 1985-1990.

[3] Maxine D. Molyneux, 'Mobilisation without Emancipation? Women's interests, state and revolution in Nicaragua' in: *Feminist Studies*, vol2, no.2, summer 1985. Updated in R. Fagan *et al* (ed): *Transition and Development: Problems of Third World Socialism*, Monthly Review Press, 1986.

[4] Rocio Palomino, *El Discrete Desencanto, una mirade al feminismo- realmente existente. El Zorro de abajo*, No.6, January 1987.

[5] The term 'terrorism' in relation to the armed action of the Communist Party of Peru (PCP), known as *Sendero Luminoso*, and of the revolutionary movement, *Tupac Amaru* (MRTA), is widespread in Peru.

[6] This has unfortunately changed, as is shown by the increasing number of murders of women organised within the poor and working-class sector since the end of 1990. During work on the Foreword, news reached us of the murder of Maria Elena Moyano, mayor of Villa El Salvador, a district of Lima, and a prominent member of the women's movement in the poor and working-class sectors. In 1991, because of her courageous pledge on behalf of the slum dwellers, she was named Personality of the Year. G.K.

Maria Amélia Teles (Brazil)

A feminist perspective on power and population control

The origins of Brazil's new women's movement are to be found in the period of military rule between 1964 and 1985. A popular movement with many different sectors developed from the mid-1970s onwards, a movement which women initially joined to fight for social improvements and to oppose the general reduction in people's purchasing power. Meanwhile, women's groups, like the the persecuted left and influential and progressive forces within the Church, demanded that the military and the security forces observe human rights and that an amnesty be granted for political prisoners. Through large-scale strikes in the late seventies the trade unions and the *Partido dos Trabalhadores* (PT), Workers' Party, which arose out of them, became driving forces behind the democratic movement.

The official end of military rule in 1985 did not lead to any break with the economic and political structures of the dictatorship. Nevertheless, new political spaces did open up for the left and spectacular election victories were achieved. Up until this point, the social movements had mainly concentrated on increasing their support through public campaigns and demonstrations. For these movements, including the feminists, a partial institutionalisation of the left presented a considerable challenge.

Is feminist work possible within institutions or does it only succeed outside patriarchal organisations? Do new developments, such as new left-wing municipal governments, open up new arenas for feminist activism or do women tend to delude themselves about the opportunities for accomplishing administrative changes?

Maria Amélia Teles has had personal experience of these contradictions. As a feminist in the *União de Mulheres de São Paulo* (Women's Union of São Paulo) and a human rights activisit in the *Commissão de Familiares de Mortos e Desaparecidos Políticos* (Association of Families of Those Murdered or Disappeared for Political Reasons) and the *Grupo Tortura Nunca Mais* (Group For No More Torture), she has been active for over ten years in autonomous organisations. She also works in the municipal government of São Paulo where the left-wing politician and former grassroots activist, Luisa Erundina, has been in power since the last elections. In the following interview she identifies some of the basic problems in the Brazilian women's movement and discusses the politics of the left-wing municipial government in São Paulo from a feminist perspective.

* * * * * * * * * *

At the Fifth Latin American and Caribbean Feminist Meeting in November 1990 in Argentina the Brazilians formed the largest group, with 700 participants. What kind of conclusions did you take home with you from this meeting?

First of all we realised at the meeting how little cohesion there is among us all. The best example of that was perhaps the opening ceremony in which each country's delegation did a joint presentation - except the Brazilians. The individual social movements and the women's movement have very little contact with each other in Brazil. Can you imagine? It was only when I saw all the indigenous women meeting in Argentina that it occurred to me that we have indigenous roots in Brazil too. But we only ever think of the European and black elements.

Is this lack of cohesion you speak of a reflection of problems or conflicts in the feminist movement or do you manage to work alongside each other quite happily?

No, we have a lot of problems. Just look at the situation in São Paulo. Ten years ago we founded the Women's Alliance. There were all kinds of women's groups in it; political parties, trade unions, independent groups etc. In 1990 we started having arguments over autonomy and our relationship to various institutions and the Alliance broke up over it. I think we should come together again and discuss this issue further. I'm optimistic that will happen.

Some of us really wanted to keep a space open for debate, so we created a Feminist Forum for Reproductive Rights. This Forum will take part in the big environmental conference. We have contact with other very similar groups in other places like Pernambuco, Rio, Minas Gerais etc. But of course the Forum isn't supposed to replace the Women's Alliance which was much broader in scope.

The other project we're trying to collaborate on is a magazine which first came out in 1991 and which is supported by six women's groups:

União de Mulheres, Colectivo Feminista de Sexualidade e Saude, the women's centres in three districts of the city and the *Centro de Informacão da Mulher*. The magazine is called *Enfoque Feminista* (Feminist Outlook). I'm telling you all this to show you just how difficult it is to work together. But, in my opinion, it's necessary.

You yourself work in the women's movement as a feminist but you also work outside it, in a project run by São Paolo's municipal government. How do you reconcile these two different political activities?

I've always been active in lots of different areas so I don't have any problems with it. I work for my living and my work has very little to do with the fact I'm a feminist. I've been working in the municipal government of São Paulo for eleven years. Of course these days I'm not just any old employee in the municipal bureaucracy because after the victory of the PT candidate, Luisa Erundina, in the city council elections, I became her political assistant. I see her victory as a very, very big victory for women in São Paulo. In the election campaign women created a women's committee to support her candidature. At that time no one wanted to back her. Even the leaders of the PT didn't want to support her. Her support came from women, especially grassroots women. The preferred party candidate was a man, but the PT grassroots spoke out against him.

After her candidature was confirmed the party withdrew completely and didn't canvass for her at all. Instead we women took to the streets and organised an election campaign for her. And why did we want her? Because she's a woman, a woman who has always struggled. She doesn't remotely resemble the cliche of a Brazilian woman who must always be young and beautiful, and a mother as well - a superwoman, in fact. Luisa is no superwoman. She's not a mother, she's never married and doesn't intend to. She's 56 years old and she's not beautiful in the traditional sense. But she's incredibly nice. She's simply exceptional. She comes from the northeast, the Brazilian poorhouse. There are many prejudices here against people from the northeast. In other words, she was the anti-candidate. Everything was against her. But we women supported her unconditionally. For me it was the first time I'd completely identified with an election campaign and enjoyed it. My decision to work directly with Luisa Erundina was the result of all that.

After her election, I was asked if I wanted to work on a newly created women's commission which was to set up a women's programme. The work was completely different from what I'd imagined. Factional politics made some of the women gang up on the women from the autonomous women's movement. That was unacceptable to me, so I spoke out against the commission, even though I'd thought at first I could contribute in the way Luisa Erundina would have done. But most things were run on the basis of party in-fighting without any participation from the grassroots. Maybe I made a mistake and should've fought for the inclusion of the women from the autonomous women's movement. But I decided to withdraw and hoped I might be able to help Luisa Erundina in another way.

What kind of work did you do then?

First I worked with so-called minority groups, with the handicapped, with blacks. Then when a secret mass grave with more than 1,000 bodies was found in Perus (a suburb of São Paulo), the municipal government decided to investigate every detail of the case, to exhume the murdered political prisoners, indentify them and prosecute the murderers. Then, of course, the bodies had to be taken back to their families so that they could be properly buried again. I did this work on behalf of a commission of inquiry into the Perus case and other mass graves.

We live in a country where impunity for murderers in state and quasi-state institutions still exists. For the first time in the history of the Brazilian government, one of its members - Luisa Erundina - spoke out against this impunity. That was a political expression of our identity. I value Luisa Erudina's action very highly. Perhaps she moves me because she's a woman, a woman from the northeast, discriminated against, and not supported by the PT. And it wasn't an easy job she took on because it meant accusing the military. That's a risky business and takes a lot of courage. I'm not sure whether a man would've done that.

What does it mean for the women of São Paulo to have a woman at the head of the municipal government?

Well, the current government has a woman's face. In some ways that's a big deal but it's still regarded as a kind of oddity as far as the press is concerned, and the population expects a lot from it. You see, the municipal government doesn't really support women, even though thousands of women live in this city and there's a feminist movement here.

How could that be achieved?

I think there were at least two basic problems which prevented that from happening. Firstly, there was a lack of political will, not from Luisa Erudina herself, but in the municipal government as a whole and also from the other women in it. Secondly the PT, consciously or unconsciously, demobilised the popular movement. The vast majority of women belong to the popular movement and after the PT entered the government these women invested more in the party than in the movement. The municipal government isn't offering any easy solutions to São Paulo's problems now. It wouldn't even have the necessary financial or political means. What they should've done is mobilise the people around existing problems to exert pressure. That was my great hope. The people who can be mobilised at the drop of a hat in São Paulo are the women; the men tag on behind. But this didn't happen and in my opinion that's a big failure.

I'd like to move onto another subject. In June, 1992, the big UN Conference for the Environment and Development (UNCED) will take place in Brazil. Will you take part in any way?

No, this conference is an official affair from start to finish. Neither the social movements nor the population as a whole are invited to participate in any way. We're organising a parallel conference with other social movements and as women we have two specific interests in it: one concerns urbanisation, the other population control. We're rejecting the official version and initiative as regards population control policies for reasons which I'll explain: allegedly the earth and her natural resources can't support a population increase. Women are tired of having babies so the rise in population must be controlled. We don't agree with this argument. Firstly, the world is wracked by an extremely unjust distribution of resources. We believe that in future everyone should share resources. Secondly, women should be able to decide for themselves whether they want to have children.

Over the last few years there's been such a massive sterilisation programme in Brazil that many women don't have this option anymore at all. Officially 25 million women have been sterilised, many of them between 15 and 19 years old. That represents a kind of preventative genocide. It really bothers us Brazilian women because it seems to us that there are many feminists in the so-called First World who support the view I've just described. They start from the principle that the earth has no more natural resources, that women don't want to have children anymore and that institutionalised birth control is the solution. But it's women who've borne the brunt of this birth control without any regard for their right to self-determination. What's more, Brazilian women have just been guinea pigs for laboratories and pharmaceutical companies developing programmes in the First World. So we know from our own experience what's behind these population control policies. It's so drastic here that in fifteen years time it's been calculated there'll be two old people for every young person. I'm sure you're aware of the official image of Brazil as a country of young, laughing people. That image just doesn't wash anymore. Until the mid-eighties half the Brazilian population was under 18. But now, in the space of a few years, the age pyramid has gone into reverse.

I also think it's crazy to carry on demanding population control policies because they've been around for a long time. In the last few years they've even had a feminist gloss with lots of PR stuff about providing integrated healthcare for women. All lies! In reality massive sterilisation has been carried out in clinics financed by the First World where there's no regard for the wishes of the women concerned, despite their claims. They also carried out experiments with hormones and dangerous drugs such as Norplant.[1] None of this reduced poverty which was the main selling-point of the population control policies, nor did it improve the quality of life or make public services more accessible or create better working conditions. In other words: birth control hasn't solved Brazil's problems. That's what we want to discuss at the parallel conference.

There are a lot of right-wing ideas around in the ecology movement. Women are held directly responsible for the ecological imbalance because they have children. This argument ignores the facts. It's not the poor who cause environmental pollution. I can see with my own eyes in my country who is polluting the environment; it's the multinationals. They destroy Amazonia, they destroy Minas Gerais. Whole mountains are excavated to mine ore.

The other issue we want to discuss at the parallel conference is urbanisation. The multinationals in Brazil today are treated like gods. For us they signify danger on the streets, fear, air pollution, and a lack of transport and infrastructure as a whole. It's always the women who have to pay first. They don't just have a double burden, they have a triple or quadruple burden to bear.

Another aspect of this is land reform which doesn't exist and poses a very serious problem for Brazil. Any solution to the problem has to begin with redistribution of the land. People are moving to the big cities because they're driven from the land. Their traditional culture is being exposed to very big changes and people find themselves in a situation once again where violence is an everyday occurrence. The number of rapes is on the increase.

So we women want to go to the conference to discuss two main issues, urbanisation and population control policies. We've already had preparatory meetings to draw up our own agenda for publication. It's clear to us that we represent a minority among the participating groups and that the feminist perspective isn't even on the agenda for most people.

Is the position of the official conference as regards population control policies something qualitatively new, in your opinion, or do you see historical continuity?

Yes, I do see historical continuity. The Brazil you see today ultimately came about because white men conquered the area and assaulted the indigenous women. So the first Brazilian women were the product of rape, that's well known. Then the Portugese brought in black slaves for cheap labour. The white men didn't behave any differently towards the black women than they had done towards the Indian women. The conquerors' policy was to populate the territory. The Portugese wanted to rule by populating the land. And what did populating mean for them? First of all they murdered the people who were already living in the country. But the new *mestizas* were not the population they wanted. There are letters written by sailors at the time who said that if it went on like this, Brazil would gradually become Africanised. So white women were brought over, irrespective of social background. In other words, a policy of population control was practised on all women, whether Indian, black or white, a policy of population control which served the colonisers, the elite, the imperialists right from the start, from 1500 right up to the present day. And they're as racist today as they were in those days. During the dictatorship a study came out which warned of the 'danger' of a black governor rising to office in 1990.

Birth control in Brazil can be legitimised by 'dangers' like these. Women's sexuality was always a function of men and the Catholic church plays an extremely negative role in this. There was never any sexual freedom for women, never any right to desire, never any right to decide freely whether they wanted to have children or not. So the right to choose is our motto and a great dream of ours.

Footnotes

[1] Norplant is a hormone contraceptive capsule inserted subcutaneously.

RECLAIMING POLITICS

María Dirlene T. Marques (Brazil)

Feminists in the Workers' Party

Preoccupation with the complex issue of power - whether at home, in official politics or within one's own group - frequently dominates discussions among organised women. Under the banner of 'participation', feminists in Peru, Mexico, Venezuela and Brazil have stood for parliament; others balk at the possibility of reforming a hierarchical system. Women with a gender perspective who get involved in mixed institutions are used to struggling for the power which they do not have. But when positive discrimination is introduced, power is actually handed over to women.

In 1980 Brazilian feminists, along with trade unionists, the urban popular movements and the Christian grassroots groups, founded the *Partido dos Trabalhadores* (PT), Workers' Party. Today this party is regarded as the most important 'New Left' party in Latin America. The founding of the PT as a left-wing party for the masses represented a break with the Leninist party model and its 'top-down', vertical structure.

With respect to the social movements, the PT claims (at least in theory) to acknowledge their autonomy and to avoid using them as front organisations or launch pads for the party. But in practice it is clear that such claims are hard to deliver and that the relationship between power and autonomy is very tense. Feminists both inside and outside the PT have had to grapple with this relationship, making a huge effort not to lose sight of their feminist aims and visions in their everyday arguments and factional struggles.

We discussed the divergence between party militancy and feminist activism with the economist, María Dirlene T. Marques, who works in the PT secretariat in Belo Horizonte.

* * * * * * * * * *

For many people in Latin America and also in Europe the PT is seen as a model party. What space do you see for women in the PT?

The PT took up office claiming to represent all marginalised people. This is a reflection of the people who founded the PT: workers, women, blacks, in a word, the oppressed of society. So the struggle for the construction of a different society is fundamental to the party's programme. As far as the position of women inside the PT is concerned, I think it's deteriorated over the last few years mainly because our women's committees went into decline when many of us decided to join the PT. You see, the women's committees didn't succeed in asserting our demands or advancing the position of women in the PT. So we came out of the movement and turned ourselves into party activists. But our original intention of getting involved in politics to advance the cause of women was pushed into the background. Although we still have women's committees on a community, regional, and national level, they're not taking much concrete action these days. To outsiders that must sound strange: but when we were involved in feminist activities, it wasn't acknowledged anywhere and didn't have any solid foundations. On the other hand, we did at least make proposals and carry them out in those days. Today we have official channels at our disposal but the flip side of the coin is that we've lost our feminist voice as a result.

What is women's representation like in the PT'S decision-making posts?

I'm the only woman out of 21 members on the regional council in Minas Gerais; on the regional executive three out of 64 members are women. The figures are similar at a national level: in the secretariat the ratio is one to 23, in the federal executive four to 83. In other words, out of every twenty leaders, there's approximately one woman.

It never used to be like that. In the early days of the PT there were many more women, many more workers and many more blacks in the leadership. But our numbers shrank as the party grew. Of course it's not only the men who are responsible for this. I think the way we women have worked in the PT has contributed to the decline in our feminist activities. There was a big discussion among us women as to whether we should develop our own programme within the PT separately from the general politics of the party or whether we should integrate ourselves into the PT structures. We chose the latter option which means each of us just do our own work in our individual areas of responsibility. In my opinion that's weakened us considerably.

Nevertheless, I genuinely believe that the PT still offers us our best chance. Inspite of everything it's possible to create a space for ourselves there. What we need to do now is claim that space, occupy it, keep completely quiet about it and then expand it. You see, we've built up a certain relationship to the party and we've come to a kind of arrangement with the men there.

Would it have been viable to leave the party instead and found an autonomous women's movement with former PT women (and others)?

No, not at this point in time. At the moment our idea is to reorganise ourselves to fight for our own space again in the PT. We need to come forward as feminist activists in the party. If we women organised ourselves, we could actually exert more pressure. We could certainly achieve more in this way than from the outside.

For several years now women in Europe have been demanding positive discrimination in political parties and in various official positions and jobs, particularly high-ranking jobs traditionally dominated by men. Is this also an issue for you?

We've been demanding positive discrimination for a long time, though until now in a rather timid, half-hearted fashion. We felt we had to earn our place first through a convincing political track record. We behaved as if were afraid of political representation and of power in general. But at the Fifth Latin America and Caribbean Feminist Meeting in November, 1990, I buried my inhibitions about this. I realised that positive discrimination is an extremely just demand. Whether we like it or not, we've got to face up to the fact that women have specific problems in the party. We sometimes turn a blind eye - it's our own party after all - but repression and discrimination do exist. By demanding positive discrimination we're openly acknowledging inequalities in the party.

Our problem is that we're organised in various different movements in the party so we have to achieve positive discrimination not only in the leadership structures of the party but also in all the various movements.[1]

Hasn't the election of someone like Luisa Erundina as mayor of São Paulo given women's work in the PT a big boost?

Yes, of course. And she's not just any woman. For us she's more of a feminist than a PT woman. She has a woman's awareness which she acts on. But I'm not always pleased to see a woman in a high position. For example, we had a woman in Collor de Melo's cabinet in charge of the Ministry of Finance, Zelia Cardoso de Melo. She was the second most important person after the President but it meant absolutely nothing to workers and even less to women. Politically she's not acceptable to us in any way, nor is she a feminist. With Luisa Erudina it's completely different.

Within the feminist debate in Latin America, some women are strictly against feminists working in the traditional parties. They argue that although they can expand the women's movement through these parties, at the same time the old power structures are simply reproduced. What do you think?

I think there's a lot of truth in that. We've come up against it ourselves, not only in the political parties but also in the feminist movement which has its own power structures and debates about independence. The traditional patriarchal models and male structures of the political parties, the left and our society as a whole are in crisis. Control, hierarchy and authoritarianism are no longer deemed necessary. This crisis could be our chance to break down the structures in the political parties and in feminism which also functions in a semi-authoritarian way, even when we *think* we've eliminated the 'above' and 'below' syndrome.

In the face of this crisis I don't know whether we have the vision or the power to create organisations with more solidarity and less authoritarianism. But to focus on the feminists for a moment, I think we're becoming increasingly political and evermore conscious of these authoritarian structures as a result. These structures could certainly carry on in their present form, that is, as authoritarian parties. But when we feminists or other people with a different perspective who are wise to this authoritarianism get involved in these parties as organised women with a different perspective, I truly believe that the first step towards change has already been taken.

Would you be interested in discussing this issue at an international or Latin American level?

The women's movement in Brazil is in an extremely bad state. There are feminists but no functioning feminist movement. Paradoxically, international meetings make us women here suddenly identify as Brazilians among all the other participants. It's then we realise just how many of us there actually are. For this reason I'm totally in favour of Latin American meetings. Mind you, many women who've been to all five of the continental feminist meetings since 1981 have concluded that ever-increasing participation is at a cost to clarity and concrete work.

Footnotes

[1] The issue of positive discrimination for women was on the agenda of the PT's National Congress in 1991. The Congress decided that there should be a minimum of 30 per cent women on all party committees.

Petrona Coronel (Paraguay)

Women leading the Paraguayan Peasants' Movement

From 1954 until 1989 Paraguayan society was dominated by the military dictator of German origin, Alfredo Stroessner. To crush any opposition, the police and security forces adopted a strategy of 'preventive repression', using arbitrary arrest, detention without trial, torture and murder. Stroessner was finally overthrown by a faction of his own army whose main concern was to secure the continued economic and political rule of the military caste and whose commitment to democracy was negligible. Nevertheless they had to grant the opposition some free scope which it used to propagate ideas about genuine democracy and social change.

What is noticeable about the various newly-founded parties and movements is the significant participation of women, particularly in positions of responsibility. Women formed about a third of the candidates of the left-wing Citizens' Union which won the first municipal elections in the capital, Asunción, in May 1991, after Stroessner's fall. In the *Movimiento Campesino Paraguayo*, Paraguayan Peasants' Movement, (MCP), eight members of the 15-strong national executive are women. The key to the high level of women's political participation lies in Paraguay's history. During the Triple Alliance War of the late nineteenth century in which Argentina, Brazil and Uruguay fought Paraguay, over ninety per cent of Paraguay's male population was killed.

After the war it was the women who rebuilt the country. Despite this contribution, women's legal status remains extremely unsatisfactory. Under a civil law passed in 1987, women are frequently described as their husbands' wards and a draft bill for the introduction of divorce was rejected by parliament. Another law gives control of matrimonial property to the husband and requires women to obtain their husbands' consent before starting paid work. The shortage of men has led to an exaggerated over-valuing of men and boys.

Under Stroessner, most of the land was carved up among a handful of

Stroessner's aides. This has left Paraguay with the most inequitable pattern of land distribution in Latin America and condemned the majority of the country's three and a half million inhabitants to poverty. Sixty per cent of all Paraguayans live in houses classified as unfit for human habitation and only seven per cent have access to safe drinking water.

Petrona Coronel from the MCP recently visited Europe as a delegate of her organisation. In the following conversation she describes the position of women both in Paraguay as a whole and in her own organisation, against this backdrop of poverty and discrimination.

* * * * * * * * * *

We have lots of visitors from Latin American organisations, including your own, but normally the MCP sends men. Was it coincidental or intentional that the MCP should send two women this time?

I'm not surprised you're interested in the make-up of our delegation. In fact there's a lot of discrimination and marginalisation in Latin America when it comes to women's political participation. Many women are discriminated against by their own husbands and their own organisations. In the MCP we've done away with this contradiction but not without a struggle. We women had to work very hard just to make our own partners more aware of their wrong attitudes. But these days I think women as well as men in the MCP recognise the importance of women's participation. On a practical level, it's now possible for women to get on in the movement. That's why I'm here instead of a man.

Do the women in the MCP have their own structures, like a women's secretariat? Or are you simply involved in the mainstream work of the organisation?

We believe both are important. I say that because I've found that women's struggle is very much determined by the social and political context of the country. If we want to resolve the many disputes affecting us *campesinas*, then in the end we have to fight for agrarian reform. It's because of the lack of it that women are so exploited, so marginalised. But we also have to raise women's specific demands alongside that, like our demand for real participation in the structures of the organisation and also at a higher level in the country's economic, political and decision-making arenas where things like agrarian reform are being discussed.

Anyway, going back to the first part of your question about the women's secretariat: the MCP is divided into five work sectors, one of which is the coordination of the *campesinas* on a regional and national level. That means there's a specific area of work concerned with women in the MCP. But we women also work in the other sectors. To give you a few figures: on the executive, three out of seven of us are women. In the national leadership we're actually in the majority: out of fifteen members, eight are women. I think that's a very significant victory, don't you?

Of course. Is this to do with the numerical strength of women in the MCP or is there a system of positive discrimination?

No, there's no such system. I think it's a reflection on all the work we women have put in. The grassroots elect a lot of women as delegates and that's repeated right up to the top.

Do you think a system of positive discrimination would be a sensible idea?

I don't think we really need that in the MCP movement. But if we were to found a political party, it'd be a different matter. In that situation I'd support it, though I wouldn't be in favour of women having a majority - I'd opt for twenty or thirty per cent. The women like a bit of a struggle!

What about at least fifty per cent?

I'd agree with that.

Are old as well as young women equally represented in the MCP?

Well, you have to bear in mind that the population of Paraguay is very young. More than fifty per cent are younger than 35 and most *campesinas* are very young. People get married at 17, 18, maybe twenty. At thirty or 33 women are already mothers with a lot of children. So would you regard them as old women?

Not in Europe. Are most Paraguayan women married or are they single mothers?

Over fifty per cent of women are single mothers, whether they're workers in the towns or *campesinas*. That's because in Paraguay *machismo* is really very marked and the system still favours men. But it also comes down to history. In the Triple Alliance War in the 1870s over ninety per cent of the men were killed so after that an overwhelming majority of the population were women. Decades later there was still a shortage of men - at home, in the schools, everywhere. And because there were so few of them around, they were pampered and given lots of privileges. On the other hand, the war meant that economic and social reconstruction was down to women. So basically, Paraguayan women have a long tradition of struggling for their rights but they also have a great deal of experience in production.

So isn't the continued existence of the machismo *you were just talking about rather a contradiction?*

No. I was talking mainly about the Paraguayan population as a whole. And you have to bear in mind that among the unorganised population in the countryside there's still a really terrible dictatorship from within, an immense discrimination. I said before that the strong female presence in the MCP today is to do with the fact that we've fought very hard - we realised that a long time ago. But succeeding was no easy matter. I think what helped us a great deal was that the MCP's starting point was the issue of class. Any man who takes that seriously also has to take on board that he cannot ruthlessly oppress women who belong to the same oppressed class. The men have gradually become conscious of this. (Laughter)

Do you believe that women in the MCP have progressed further than women in Paraguay as a whole?

Yes, I do, and there's living proof of that. Quite apart from the fact that the MCP is the only organisation in the country that has its own women's sections, the team of *campesinas* which co-ordinates the sections has been shown to be one of the strongest organisations around. It can mobilise across the country more effectively than anyone else. We're renowned for coming forward with concrete proposals, often jointly with organised workers, particularly in Asunción.

How many women are there in the MCP?

Well, I can't give you the exact figures because at the moment we're still busy trying to register the members properly. We've got something like 100,000 members, about half of which are women.

Do you have good contact with other women's organisations in Paraguay?

Yes, particularly some of the trade unions, like the textile trade union in Asunción, commercial employees and nurses. We have joint meetings with them and we belong to the Trade Union Confederation, CUT.

Are there joint campaigns?

Yes, of course. To give you an example, we collaborated in the creation of a women's section when the CUT was founded. Now there's a women's secretariat there too.

You just said that women in the MCP have made more progress and are more aware than other women in Paraguay. But is there any sort of common women's consciousness in society at large? Or do Paraguayan women identify more with their own respective social classes?

I think some things have changed recently and we've achieved a great deal. After the fall of the Stroessner dictatorship the consciousness of female workers in the urban trade unions took a great leap forward. They became aware of how important political participation is and how vital individual space is to gain further rights. A lot of women's groups have been founded recently. I don't just mean feminist groups which only demand women's rights. On the other hand, I feel that the struggle of Paraguayan women still needs to be taken a lot further. We must have political and economic change.

So you don't describe yourselves as feminists?

Feminists... no, but that doesn't mean we avoid raising demands which only affect us as women and which we can only achieve as women. It's just that we don't limit ourselves to that. We're clear that we're fighting for something more global and we know that our men are also exploited. All those who are oppressed should take part in this struggle.

Let me just stick with feminism for a moment longer. How would you describe feminists? Women who are only concerned with women's issues? Is that why you don't see yourselves as feminists?

Yes, precisely. For example, there are women's groups we call bourgeois who only make feminist demands, like the freedom to leave the house and come back whenever a woman wants, without her husband making the decision, like he's always done up to now. That seems ridiculous to us. A *campesina* is never locked up at home, in any case. But as *campesinas* we suffer a much more serious daily exploitation. That's why we don't limit ourselves to these rather superficial, sentimental demands which we call feminist.

Isn't it also a struggle against the reduced presence of women the higher you go up the institutional and state hierarchy?

Absolutely. But since Stroessner's time there've been some changes even at the top levels which used to be out of bounds to women. In those days, there were no female members of parliament at all, let alone female ministers. Today, the Ministry of Health is headed by a woman.

Is there any collaboration between yourselves and these women? What do you expect of these women working in a partiarchal structure?

Absolutely nothing. They work in a social and economic structure whose interests are not ours. So there's practically no chance of that happening, even if you wanted it to. These women work in a capitalist organisation so their aims are inevitably within its terms of reference.

Paraguay is a very Catholic country. Do women have problems with the Catholic hierarchy when you raise your demands?

There are problems for the women on a personal level over the number of children they have. Maybe after their late twenties women don't want to have any more children. But the Church forbids contraception which means it's not acceptable to the women either. Maybe that's why the conflict between the Church and the population still hasn't reached its climax. But I think the young women have a more realistic attitude. The older women's attitudes simply have to be changed. Who can still look after ten, twelve or even thirteen children in this day and age? Contraception is a necessity, it's common sense.

Ideally, how many children should each women in Paraguay have?

Three, in view of the critical economic situation.

Are contraceptives available?

Oh, yes. I suspect that wealthy countries, especially the US, are flooding Latin America with them on purpose. They see the population in the South increasing and in their mind the growing workforce is superfluous. So contraceptives are freely available here.

Are they expensive?

That depends on the type of contraceptive. What is worrying is that women use contraceptives without any recommendations from a doctor or any supervision. This often leads to serious side effects.

Do men also use contraceptives?

You can buy whatever you want on the free market.

I can imagine that for men in a macho *society condoms might be unthinkable...*

Yes, that's often true but worse still: in many cases, men forbid women to use contraceptives. I'm not kidding!

Is that true of MCP men? Do you talk about it?

We've discussed this problem in the MCP youth group, with women and men. But I've already told you that many of the somewhat older women have big problems themselves with this subject. In the women's group there are completely differing opinions about the use of contraceptives. To avoid getting bogged down in arguments, we tend to by-pass the subject.

Could you say something about the division of labour in the countryside where the MCP has its base?

Women have a heavier workload than men. A *campesina* gets up at three o'clock in the morning, does the housework, makes the children's school dinner and usually goes to the fields after that. Those who stay at home look after the animals.

What's your own day like?

I still live with my parents so I don't have as many problems as women who live with their men and their own children. But I also do a lot of housework apart from my work in the regional MCP office. Fortunately, everyone in my family is very politically active; my brothers, my parents - we're all members of the MCP.

Do your brothers also do housework?

Yes, I'm the only daughter and the eldest. My brothers help a lot as well. The younger generation certainly have different ideas in this respect.

You work at a regional level in the education sector. Do you run special programmes for girls and women?

Basically the educational content of the programmes is the same for men as it is for women. But we do cover special themes like 'children's rights' and 'political participation' and we run a whole range of educational and health programmes with the women's co-ordinating team. Education is actually a woman's realm in our communities. Teaching in schools is also done by women.

I'm a bit unsure as to whether or not you think there are specific women's demands which women should fight for on their own without men.

There are none, really, so long as the men think the same way as us and appreciate our importance. But that's where it comes unstuck: regarding participation, we have to keep them on their toes to stop them discriminating against us.

The MCP is participating in the Latin American campaign against the 500 year Columbus anniversary celebrations. What part is it playing?

The MCP is part of the coordinating committee for the southern cone of Latin America. We're responsible for organising various activities designed to create awareness about the origins of foreign exploitation and the rape of the continent. Young women and the Organisation of Families of the Disappeared and Murdered, which is mainly female, are particularly in these activities. The Families are involved mainly because 12 October is the day their organisation was founded - the day all the killing and torture began, as well as the anniversary of Columbus' arrival.

Does that mean the women have a particular interest in this campaign?

Yes. Our starting point is that the Indian women suffered the most from the arrival of the Spanish, physically as well as economically. We're working on a whole list of demands and are cooperating closely with the women from the Organisation of Families of the Disappeared and Murdered, mainly in the area of human rights. We're holding human rights seminars to raise consciousness about why we should continue the work for which our colleagues were disappeared or murdered in the first place. The MCP Youth is preparing massive festivities in the different regions to mark this date. We feel that our culture, our dance, our common way of life was raped and suppressed on 12 October.

You raised the subject of those who were disappeared or murdered. Do you have any information regarding overtly sexual methods of repression against women?

The ones who were disappeared were mainly men. But just as many women as men ended up in prison because they both took part in the struggle. I know many women who suffered severe torture in prison. There are lots of cases of sexual torture.

Claudia Colimoro (Mexico)

A prostitute's election campaign

On 16 March 1991, the *Convención Nacional de Mujeres por la Democracia*, National Women's Convention For Democracy, was founded in Mexico - a startling achievement at a time when Mexican feminists everywhere were lamenting the splintering of their movement. Not since the 1930s, when a broad women's front campaigned for women's suffrage, had there been any comparable women's association which aimed to intervene in official politics on a women's ticket. The Convention was founded in the run-up to the parliamentary and municipal elections on 18 August 1991. It proposed that the political parties accept female candidates onto their lists, candidates who explicitly wanted to raise women's demands in parliament. Some of the left-wing parties were willing to do this. From a mathematical point of view, the initiative was a failure; only three candidates from the Convention were elected. This was largely due to the fact that the left-wing parties suffered severe losses across the board and only won a handful of parliamentary seats altogether. But the habitual election-rigging master-minded by the ruling party, the PRI, also played its part in the poor results.

Nevertheless, the women in the Convention did not see the election results as a disaster. The simple fact that all the political parties had had to discuss whether they wanted to give places to women on their lists signified an invasion of male bastions, especially at a time of cutbacks in the state-financed bureaucracy and economy, when women's position in the workforce was under threat. What proved extremely difficult was firstly the search for common ground with the public and secondly the negotiations over concrete political programmes.

One of the candidates for the Mexico City parliament was Claudia Colimoro, a feminist prostitute, who was on the Revolutionary Workers' Party (PRT) slate. During the run-up to the elections, there was a Mexican women's convention on the theme 'Whom does politics belong to?'.

During the convention it was stated that a sexual contract which reinforces the sexual hierarchy in society precedes the social contract. If that is so, then Claudia Colimoro's candidature was a particularly disruptive force: she struck a blow at the very foundations of the patriarchal order. The following report by Claudia provides an insight into the subject of women and violence.

* * * * * * * * * *

I am 35 years old and have three children. I began working as a prostitute when I was a secretary in the social welfare office. At that time I was in financial straits because one of my children was ill. I worked over twelve hours a day in the office and also had to satisfy my boss's sexual desires just to keep my job. I soon realised that I could earn considerably more money as a prostitute.

Four and a half years ago I got involved in the fight against AIDS. We needed to teach the other girls about the causes and consequences of this dreadful illness. It was very difficult work and we had no money and no support from official institutions. We founded the citizens' alliance, CUILOTZIN, which fights for healthcare and civil rights for prostitutes of both sexes and street children. CUILOTZIN organises educational meetings about AIDS and protection against it. We work with the National Anti-AIDS Association (CONASIDA) which also gives us condoms for free distribution among the prostitutes. Now the girls refuse to go with a client who won't use a condom. We've had very good results and as vice-president of CUILOTZIN, I was even visited by representatives of the World Health Organisation (WHO). Thanks to our efforts there is now a clinic which deals with the health problems of prostitutes and regularly examines them - not only to detect the AIDS virus as early as possible, but also Hepatitis B and other sexual diseases. The clinic carries out free gynocological and pregnancy examinations for prostitutes and free operations for them and their children. CUILOTZIN also cares for domestic servants who have been sexually molested or beaten by their employers.

We are fighting to gain recognition of prostitutes' rights and the legalisation of their trade. The situation which forces them to break the law over and over again reflects society's bigotry and double standards. It simply means the girls can be unscrupulously exploited and oppressed by officials. In Mexico prostitution is 'regulated' by laws passed 56 years ago which are now completely out of date. Prostitution is illegal and pushed underground which means that prostitutes have no rights whatsoever. They would be in a much better position if their profession were legally recognised. Their individual earnings would appreciate by paying taxes because they would not have to surrender money unconditionally to corrupt officials and police. The legalisation of prostitution would also make it possible to control AIDS more effectively. Current AIDS legislation is really nothing more than the syphilis law passed in 1934 in which that word has simply been replaced with 'AIDS'. After the charges we brought, a law has now been passed whereby people who slander prostitutes and exploit them can be fined, fired or even sentenced to jail.

Brutal Attacks by the Right

We've also managed to organise creches for prostitutes who work during the day. In November 1990, after a discussion between the prostitutes' representatives and officials from the Ministry of Health, the *Provida* movement (right-wing upholders of morality) destroyed two creches for prostitutes. They still exist inspite of these attacks, but in places which are only known to the prostitutes.

At the moment we're working on a project for street children. They have to survive by selling or trading little odds and ends and are particularly susceptible to prostitution and drugs. We don't want them to end up in those barbarous children's homes. We hope to set up canteens, an overnight shelter and free training for them so that they'll find it easier to get normal jobs.

We have a similar project for prostitutes. We want to teach them sewing, mending clothes and other skills to help them find well-paid work when they give up their current trade through age or fatigue. Women in Mexico work for starvation wages. In the border areas, for example, women in the *maquiladoras* (foreign-owned assembly plants) work 15 hours a day and still don't earn enough to cover the cost of living. They have to work as prostitutes at the weekend. That's true of about half of them. So long as they're paid such low wages, without any proper social services or creches, women will continue to turn to prostitution in order to feed themselves and their children. Ninety-five per cent of prostitutes are mothers.

Mud Slinging

As I'm also a feminist, I took part in the National Assembly of Women for Democracy. This united forty organisations, movements and women's associations. The assembly proposed me as a candidate for the elections and began to look for a political party which would take me onto their slate. We suffered many setbacks but the PRT and the Socialist Election Front (FES) accepted immediately. It cost them votes and provoked violent attacks from the right, especially the ultra-conservative Party of National Action (PAN) and the *Provida* movement. They reacted against my demands for the liberalisation of anti-abortion laws, quite apart from my calls for the legalisation of prostitution, a systematic campaign against AIDS and universal sex education. *Provida* churned out photos of a completely mangled, eight-month foetus and described me as an 'abortionist' along with other feminist candidates of the PRT, like Rosario Ibarra.

Working with the PRT was very important to me because, even though I'm not a member, I do agree with many points in their manifesto: self-determination as regards sexuality, the right to organise, the campaign against violence against women, democratic rights, legalisation of abortion and the return of the disappeared.

My election campaign was very difficult. At first the journalists treated me amicably and compared me affectionately to 'La Cicciolina' [1]. Later on they realised I was running a serious campaign and was quite determined to make myself heard, to commit myself to the legalisation of prostitution and break the power of the corrupt authorities. After that I was bitterly attacked because I said loud and clear that every woman on this planet could end up being a prostitute and that wealth and snow-white clothing only serve to veil the fact that a woman belongs to a man sexually.

During the election campaign I got a good overview of the situation and the needs of prostitutes throughout the country. Recently, for example, I protested against two police raids in Queretaro in which lots of girls and transvestites were arrested, undressed and smeared with paint. We make a stand against these repeated attacks by the authorities in red light districts. Prostitutes are citizens just like anyone else. In Mexicali prostitutes are taken to a health centre every fortnight where they get a massive dose of some kind of penicillin, even when they don't have any infectious, sexually-transmitted diseases. That weakens their bodies' resistance. In the federal state of Sonora, the health authority insisted that for AIDS tests people had to give their name, address and date of birth, even though AIDS tests are supposed to be anonymous, secret and free. Only after a considerable struggle did we manage to stop this practice recently. When I went to a meeting in Baja California, in northwest Mexico, a conservative newspaper in Tijuana wrote that the PRT filled their ranks with prostitutes and AIDS-infested homosexuals.

This was the first time a prostitute had stood as a candidate in an election in Mexico and it's obvious that I received a lot of votes from women. The election rigging by the ruling PRI, however, was so extreme that we failed to win any seats at all. At the polling station where my son and I cast our votes in front of some journalists, the PRT didn't receive a single vote at the count... I wanted to win to put an end to the horror stories and the double standards in the media and to make ourselves heard. I am a voice for those who have none.

First printed in *Inprekorr* 241

Footnotes

[1] Ilona Staller, Italian porno queen and member of parliament for the left-wing liberal *Partito Liberale*, revealed in her election campaign the prudery and double standards of Italian society by her provocative and flamboyant appearances. Her candidature was basically a media stunt.

María Teresa Blandón (Nicaragua)

The impact of the Sandinista defeat on Nicaraguan feminism

No other women's movement in Latin America has aroused as much international attention as Nicaragua's. With the victory of the Sandinista revolution over the dictator, Somoza, in July 1979, and the creation of the *Asociación de Mujeres Nicaraguenses Luisa Amanda Espinoza* (AMNLAE), the Luisa Amanda Espinoza Nicaraguan Women's Association, as an organisation of revolutionary women, there was a general hope that a giant step had been taken towards women's liberation. But AMNLAE did not develop into a feminist organisation: it remained an outreach organisation of the ruling *Frente Sandinista de Liberación Nacional* (FSLN), Sandinista Front for National Liberation, and in the following years its main programme limited itself to traditional women's work for the Party, with the mothers of those killed in action, for example, or with housewives active in the neighbourhood committees. However, an active and multi-faceted women's movement developed parallel to AMNLAE, partly in response to the fact that patriarchal structures had remained untouched and the traditional image of women was still maintained.

This women's movement had an innovative critique of the social fabric and gave the social debates a fresh impulse. While these self-declared feminists did not encounter much support from many Sandinistas, they had influential platforms at their disposal in the pro-Sandinista media and the women's secretariats of the trade unions and other mass organisations, through which they could intervene and disseminate their views. In the late 1980s AMNLAE also tried to turn itself into a more open movement but most women activists were no longer prepared to acknowledge AMNLAE'S claim to leadership.

The FSLN's election defeat on 25 February 1990 changed the direction of the Nicaraguan women's movement. The deterioration in living conditions, already noticeable from the mid-eighties onwards, has continued unabated. Added to this is the ideological regression under the current conservative president, Violeta Chamorro.

María Teresa Blandón worked for a long time in the women's secretariat of the *Asociación de Trabajadores del Campo* (ATC), the agricultural workers' union, and organised Nicaragua's first feminist meeting in January 1992. Here she describes the position of Nicaraguan feminists, their conflicts with the FSLN and the preparations for the feminist meeting. The following essay was written on the eve of this highly successful event which has had a significant impact on women's movements throughout Central America ever since.

* * * * * * * * * *

I know that the development of the Nicaraguan women's movement has already been analysed in a hundred different ways over the past ten years by women both inside and outside the country. So I shall simply make one fundamental precursory remark: the women's movement like other social movements is also a product of the FSLN's revolution. In their first social programme there were no slogans about gender-specific oppression but a number of women in the lower ranks of the FSLN soon recognised this as a crucial issue. In the years to follow, they took on the task of developing gender-specific perspectives within the national women's organisation, AMNLAE.

The presence of Latin American and European feminists in the country at that time and their exchange of experiences with Nicaraguans no doubt played its part. Equally the participation of many of us in various different women's meetings was also a factor. Such events enabled us to develop a new programme and political praxis, which on the one hand recognised the close connection between the popular movement and the women's movement and, on the other, respected the uniqueness of the women's movement. We realised that even in our revolutionary society a form of oppression and discrimination existed in our daily as well as our public lives which was tacitly accepted because cultural values presented it as 'normal'. We women soon realised we would have to wage various struggles which might not be supported by our 'fellow travellers'. What we needed was an alliance based on a consensus of and for women in order to develop our social perspectives.

Since 1987 we have been trying to secure our own autonomous space from which to launch ourselves as genuine political protagonists. For us that doesn't just mean carrying out various actions but also participating under equal conditions in the decision-making process. Let me give you a few examples to illustrate my point.

In the past women in mixed organisations hardly ever rose to leadership positions, even when our work was of great value - for example, in the trade unions. If a woman did finally get there, she found herself constantly in the minority and was under extreme pressure not to broach any subjects related to women. We had to make a real effort to get so-called 'women's issues' onto organisations' agendas. Despite the efforts of some women over the past few years, at National Assembly level there was never any success in getting laws against violence against women passed or maintenance laws satisfactorily amended. Neither was there a reform of the penal law in which a woman is still regarded as her parents' possession for as long as she is single. After marriage she passes into the possession of the husband. Moreover, the issue as to who has the power of disposal over material and financial property has not been resolved either.

The non-governmental organisations managed to get mixed organisations to acknowledge that we women have the right to a full legal, contractual status and to develop initiatives to address our most pressing problems. Similarly, we Nicaraguan feminists strove to change the political programme of the FSLN. As a result, in the political arena we were considered radical, sectarian and influenced by foreign ideas. Naturally this enabled the more conservative female leaders to describe themselves as more revolutionary than us and their status remained intact.

Perseverance

All this is part of our most recent history. Regarding the political changes in our country brought on by the 1990 elections, I would say they have had a double effect on the women's movement. In one respect the effects were negative because what we had once achieved and what we thought was secure and lasting, is now under threat. Unemployment among women has risen to over seventy per cent, many nurseries and women's health and educational programmes have been shut down and both the old and new mass media revived their former practice of exploiting the female body commercially. In its religious discourse as well as in educational texts the church hierarchy legitimised the views of those who are now in authority on educational matters, promoting a conservative, hypocritical and discriminatory morality whose purpose is to push women back into their traditional role as mother, wife and an object of beauty pleasing to men.

This avalanche of regression hit the women's movement hard; the first reaction was defensive. 1990 was a year of re-thinking, of shock, a sad year. This phase fortunately passed quite quickly, because at the end of the year and for the whole of 1991 we responded with a clear analysis of what we wanted as women, without allowing ourselves to be deceived or trapped by the pressing problems of the situation. We managed to identify our most urgent, strategic needs. In August 1990 the former AMNLAE leadership, the women's secretariats of various associations and trade unions (which already saw themselves as more or less autonomous), women's groups, women's centres and independent women, all tried to instigate a process of reflection with interested women from the various sectors about two different issues: firstly, about women's most pressing problems and our proposed solutions and, secondly, about the state of the women's movement and how we viewed our past experiences. Recognising our various differences was an absolute prerequisite for this process, enabling us to achieve better forms of organisation and a greater capacity to mobilise people.

The 52 Per Cent Festival

This process lasted until February 1991 when AMNLAE decided to have its own meeting on 8 March at which the main points in their future programme would be drawn up. On this occasion it also elected its new leadership, headed by Gladys Baez, a Sandinista activist with many years' experience of struggle. The rest of the women who had participated in the process until then celebrated 8 March with a festival of the so-called 52 per cent, a reference to the percentage of women in the population. The festival lasted three days and demonstrated a new way of coming together. We wanted to show society who we were, what we were doing, what problems we were faced with, what we were thinking and what demands we were making.

Like so many other initiatives the Festival was exposed to attacks from extreme conservative groups who tried to discredit us by calling us lesbians and anti-Sandinistas. Relatively few women actually took part but it had a very positive political effect on women from the different sectors. As a result of this public break with AMNLAE, the women's secretariats of the trade unions who still considered themselves part of AMNLAE, declared their own autonomy. They gave the following reasons for their differences with AMNLAE:

- A rigid way of working, commitment to issues which didn't always relate to the reality of women in the respective sectors.

- A lack of recognition of different interests, experiences and leadership roles.

From March 1991 to January 1992 we concentrated on the preparation of a national women's meeting to which we invited 500 women from different social sectors and regions of the country. Plurality and the differences between us are the guiding principles for this meeting; it will pave the way for a new type of future which no longer consists of representation of thousands by the very few. Every individual contribution is significant to us. The meeting will further our interest in getting to know each other, exchanging thoughts and experiences and developing common proposals for action to change the relationship between men and women. The preparations have been difficult. The national leadership of AMNLAE, the ATC and the *Central Sandinista de Trabajadores* (CST)[1], the Sandinista trade union confederation representing industrial workers, decided not to take part, without giving any solid political arguments or explanations. This greatly concerned us. We tried in vain to engage in some sort of dialogue but sectarianism and fear of political debate prevailed. Despite these complications, we achieved sufficient support for our Nicaraguan women's meeting to go ahead in January 1992 in Managua.

The conference slogan is: 'Unity in Diversity' and its aims are as follows: firstly, an exchange of experiences between the different groups who work with women's problems; secondly, an analysis of the effects of current economic policies on women's living conditions and an appropriate response; and thirdly, the planning of joint actions. Accordingly, we've chosen six main issues which all the participants should consider and discuss. Firstly, as I've said, the effects of economic policies on women's daily lives and work, experiences in connection with these and an assessment of the solutions. Secondly, methods and aims of organising women. How can we protect the political spaces we have won and open up new ones? Thirdly, health and reproductive policies. Fourthly, violence against women - the causes and our action to oppose it. Fifth, relationships and sexuality. Sixth, popular culture and its role models of discrimination against women and forms of action for a non-discriminatory and anti-sexist education and culture.

We hope that this meeting - the first of its kind - will lead to a *rapprochement* between the variously organised women, our successful autonomous mobilisation for specific action and issues on the basis of mutual interest, while respecting the differences between us and thus also strengthening our communality. We know that it is possible and therefore we look to the future with courage and hope.

Footnotes

[1]The CST is a Sandinista trade union confederation mainly representing industrial workers.

Carolina Aguilar and Alicia Chenard (Cuba)

Is there a place for feminism in the revolution?

Following the 1959 revolution, socialist Cuba was considered a model for many political and social movements in Latin America. An economic development programme was introduced and a model health and educational system was developed; basic social security was also achieved. Numerous improvements were also brought about for women; protection against unfair dismissal, free distribution of contraceptives, legalisation of abortion, childcare in creches, kindergartens and full day schools among others. Women are well represented in the labour force and a sex education programme has been implemented which promotes equal rights.

The reverse side of the Cuban development model is an impenetrable bureaucratic power machine which steers the country from above and regiments public life. In the eyes of most Cuban women, the mass organisations - Committees for the Defence of the Revolution (CDR), Youth Organisation (UJC), Women's Organisation (FMC) - are simply branches of the Party rather than autonomous organisations designed to formulate their demands. But unlike the former socialist countries of Eastern Europe, development has never been static in Cuba. Contrary to the anti-Cuban propaganda promoted by the US, changes are not taboo and in the mass organisations there are open discussions about the failings of the revolution in meeting women's needs. There is a general feeling that 'adjustments' are necessary. This is also true of the Cuban Women's Federation, FMC, which is slowly and carefully responding to the various impulses and debates of the feminist movement in Latin America and is seeking a new definition for its work.

Carolina Aguilar is the former managing editor of the periodical, *Mujeres*, (Women) and a member of the national leadership of the FMC in Havana. Alicia Chenard works there in the department of foreign affairs.

* * * * * * * * * *

Apart from the burning issue of economic survival, there are more and more discussions in the mass organisations on internal democratisation. Is there a debate about this in the FMC?

Carolina: Well, there've been serious discussions for quite a long time now - since 1986 and the Third Party Congress - about how to bring about change or 'rectification' in all the country's institutions, starting with the Communist Party right down to all the mass movements. The rectification process is supposed to be economic but it's also political: mistakes and negative tendencies which had crept in needed to be rectified. The aim was to improve socialism, our socialism. Obviously our organisation is involved in this process. But in relation to women there's another issue: after the Third Communist Party Congress we had our own congress, the fourth, which prescribed the same process. I'd say that was no coincidence. Quite the opposite, these realisations are the result of the development of one and the same society, the fruits of the revolution, of experiences on an individual as well as a social level. But I'll stick to to the Federation for now, because I know that best.

What are the most pressing issues for the Federation at the moment?

Carolina: The FMC was thirty years old in 1990. For the past two years we've been in a process of collective reflection and analysis which is still going on. Why? Because Cuban women are not the same as they were thirty years ago. On the other hand, the Federation is still the same, with the same aims it set out with. It still concentrates on making sure that women can exercise the rights that are owed them - rights secured by the socialist revolution. There can be no socialist revolution without complete equality and justice between both men and women and also between races. The process whereby a woman becomes a free and equal being is an extremely complex one. It touches on her areas of work and family, but also her mentality, which is a very difficult sphere, not to mention her consciousness of society. Thirty years is a short time for something like that. But nevertheless, women's situation has changed.

You said that changes have been discussed within the FMC for the past two years. What has changed since then?

Carolina: To answer that properly I have to go back a bit. In the course of time, women have changed, as I said. They think and live differently today. We have statistical proof of that. In 1959 twelve per cent of the workforce were women. Today they are 39 per cent and in some parts of the country, such as the capital, Havana, they are 47 per cent of the workforce. In 1960 and 1961 we had to fight for literacy. By contrast, women today make up 58 per cent of the qualified workforce, i.e. skilled workers, technicians, engineers and so on. In those days it was unthinkable that women could be scientists; today a quarter of Cuban scientists are women. In other words, women today are an educated force, not only in relation to school and professional education, but also educated in the sense of having developed their own thoughts and recognised the opportunities offered by socialism.

The grassroots work of the Federation has to take this situation into account. For example, we dissolved the Federation's action groups in the factories in 1974 after the Second Congress because the trade unions could take over their work. You see, as more and more women joined the workforce the trade unions had to understand the problems of working women and discuss them. Forty or fifty of us women from the National Leadership are meeting every evening at the moment to reflect on our future work. The basic question is: what can the Federation offer women today? You see, women who've reached a certain point in their lives are showing less and less interest in the Federation these days. There's nothing more to motivate them to come. Workers say: I have my work, what more can they tell me about the importance of being part of production? What's the problem?

The problem is that we have brought about the participation of women in the revolution and they have discovered their own abilities. But now we're at the next stage - the hub of the problem: women are integrated into social production, but men aren't integrated into reproduction. Men avoid reproduction within the family. Women continue to carry the burdens consigned to them historically, which are nothing other than a social construction. They are responsible for housework, for bringing up the children, basically for all the cultural, educational and economic functions within the family where the entire workforce and life itself are reproduced. That means they work outside and in the home. They have a double working day.

We have to change this situation in two ways: one way concerns the material aspect. In principle we are happy with the view of the party and the government that the appropriate institutions and services have to be created and guaranteed. The state itself must declare itself responsible for an essential part of housework, for looking after the children, for caring for the elderly, for education. Basically that is all guaranteed and the appropriate institutions have been created, though far too few of them. We have day-nurseries for children up to six, we have senior citizens clubs, but just not enough of them, because of the country's economic straits. The solution lies in informing people about the situation, changing awareness and the culture. And there's a lot still to be done. You read about many wonderful things in newspapers and magazines but in daily life everything is terribly difficult.

In the Federation we consider one thing to be fundamental: to change women's awareness so that they're actually able to lay claim to their right to equality. In other parts of the continent people talk of gender-specific awareness. That's precisely what our current task is all about: to create a gender-specific awareness in women. There can be any number of laws concerning the family but if women themselves aren't convinced they can benefit from them, then nothing will change. We call this stage the stage of revolution within the family.

Alicia: We must do things differently from before and adapt our work more to the different age groups.

Carolina: There are many structural problems with our work with girls. Thousands of girls spend their upper school years in the country because of our system of combined learning and working. Naturally there are no FMC groups there. Instead, the girls are organised in the Schoolgirls' Federation. You'd think this Federation might address girls' and women's problems. Not a bit of it! There's still a lot to do there. Many schoolgirls and students are not at all conscious of their role as women. Sometimes we feel really bad when we see students and women in technical professions. They've had all the opportunities for professional qualification. They feel they have equal rights and treat us in a rather condescending manner because they have no idea what we want. They think everything has been achieved and there's nothing more that needs fighting for. Two errors are at the root of this: firstly, we in the Federation have paid too little attention to the girls' sector. Secondly, there's a problem with the education system itself. I don't mean just the official education system, but above all the youth organisations. Here I have to criticise the UJC, although basically we work very well together. They should do much more on women's issues.

Alicia: The other problem is adult women. Quite a few have achieved power, but only in the public domain, not in the private. And yet a woman's workload in the family hinders her ability to achieve equality. For example, it prevents her from putting herself forward for the *Poder Popular* (Cuban parliament) as readily as her husband might.

Carolina: Our new attitudes towards our various tasks make it impossible to continue talking about women *en masse*. We have to differentiate between ages and professions and offer something for elderly women. Let's not forget that women's life expectancy is now 76. And finally we also have to work with the girls who neither go to school or work. This is something we do have here, as is so often the case in under-developed countries. It reflects the backwardness of the provinces compared to the capital.

On the other hand, we also have to cater for intellectual women and those at university. We are working with the UNEAC and the Media Association and we're doing some very interesting work with the universities: in the town of Villaclara we've created a professorial chair for women's studies in the department of higher education. And in the university of Havana the first professorial chair for women's studies is currently being created. It's an interdisciplinary professorial chair and a number of faculties are involved, from the economics faculty to the medical, right across to the social sciences faculty.

What sort of status will this subject have? Will it be studied in conjunction with other subjects or will it be a course in its own right?

Carolina: The main aim is to open up new areas of study. The professors are supposed to supply us with their knowledge and expertise for new projects such as women's training centres.

Male or female professors?

Carolina: Both. Similarly, the students will be of both sexes. The great thing in Cuba is that we can combine practical and academic work. The most fundamental and important task which lies ahead of us is to create a gender specific awareness.

What does this mean for the day-to-day work of the FMC?

Carolina: Well, that's a very difficult question. You see, in the early days we were busy creating an awareness among women of the significance of their own work. Today women are integrated into social production. They're totally accepted and not discriminated against. Their position in the workforce is stable - over the last five years 98 per cent of women's jobs were stable. The percentage is much higher than with men.

Why is that, in your opinion?

Carolina: You know, if a woman becomes economically independent through her job, if she can broaden her horizons and her expectations for the future through it, then she defends those achievements and she keeps her job.

Are men different? Are they less reliable?

Carolina: Men are more mobile. I wouldn't say they were less reliable. They're very restless, they want to change professions, find a better job, preferably in Havana today and in another town tomorrow, just for the sake of it, even when it turns out in the end that the new job isn't any better. And another thing, women do better at their school leaving exams and at university. They're better pupils and students, they're tougher and more persistent. I see it like this: if women are freed from repression and capitalist exploitation, then all the negative attributes attached to them in the past turn into positive ones. So women's heritage of repression actually means they are more disciplined. This is reflected in their work, their studies and also in defence: women in the militia are much more disciplined, much more enthusiastic and much more motivated than their male colleagues.

From what you're saying, it seems to me that women in Cuba are much more important and stronger than men. Surely this must scare men?

Carolina: Well, I wouldn't put it quite like that. But, in my view, women in Cuba are more closely tied to the revolution than men; they're more complete revolutionaries because they've gained more through the revolution than men. For example, in their awareness as women, in the awareness of their equality and of their rights they've come further than men.

We regard *machismo* as a residue of a repressive, *macho* culture which we've dragged along with us since time immemorial, a characteristic of all former capitalist societies and brought here by the Spanish 500 years ago. Basically, they gave us a regime of feudal slavery - there were still slaves in Cuba in 1868. The slaves worked in agriculture, in the cane fields. Two societies existed alongside one another, the feudal one and the exploitation of the slaves. The neo-colonial capitalism of more recent times followed on from there. We were nothing but a branch office of the US. The culture which grew out of this, the perceptions about men's and women's roles are still very deeply rooted. We women sometimes fall into the same trap ourselves, when these perceptions cause discrimination against women, perhaps in a joke or in behaviour on the street. We laugh or act like 'the little woman' and only see through our own stereotypical behaviour when it's too late.

What are your views on the term, 'feminism'?

Carolina: Well, first of all, when the Federation was founded and we began to work with women, we concentrated on practical work. We never used the term, feminism, in our work. At that time we were caught up with the needs of the country and the revolution. We wanted to provide support for women so that they not only received an education and enjoyed equality, but were also actively integrated into the political process. I admit that until a few years ago we did have certain prejudices against feminism, no doubt also because feminism internationally is divided into so many different tendencies. Today this sceptical phase has been more or less overcome. We enjoy very good relations with the feminist movement. We can truly say that feminism as a theory has made valuable contributions to the women's movement. On the other hand, we Cubans have devoted ourselves to practical work. We haven't developed any theory like feminism has done.

What do you think feminism has achieved?

Alicia: We can only speak from our own experiences. I think we still have a long way to go before we can talk of a feminist movement in Cuba but I think the feminist movement in our country has already contributed a great deal.

Are there Cuban women who describe themselves explicitly as feminists?

Alicia: As I've already said, we have to liberate ourselves from our prejudices against the word 'feminism'. I mean if you look back at the history of Cuban women before the revolution, you'll find that the first women who fought for the emancipation of their sex called themselves feminists. And basically what was this feminism? The struggle for women's rights. So I don't think we should be afraid of the word but we don't actually use the term here.

Not even today?

Alicia: No. Not because of any particular prejudices but because it has simply never been used. Having said that, it is gradually being introduced.

Is feminism often discussed in the Federation or does everyone just have their own thoughts about it?

Carolina: No, it's discussed, though only after the fundamentals have been explained. Alicia just said that we don't use the term, feminism, but in fact we do use it with our good friends abroad who are feminists and whose views we support.

How do you regard the relationship between Marxism and feminism?

Carolina: The first thing I have to say is that Marx did not ignore the subject of women's emancipation. We have built on his thoughts and developed our own attitude towards equality and equal rights for women. Our interpretation and our application of the theories have been developed with reference to our own criteria so we don't always find ourselves in harmony with other Marxists. We deeply regret that some Marxist parties have failed to make women's issues their own and act as if socialism in itself can solve the whole problem.

Why do you think they evade women's issued? Because they haven't read their Marx thoroughly enough or because in these parties it's men who are in charge?

Carolina: I think the main reason is patriarchy. In other words, parties are led by men who've lost touch with the original context, because in the Russian revolution women had an incredibly important role to play. In the early years of the revolution there were serious debates about this which were still going on when Lenin died. I only remember Clara Zetkin. Male historians have simply identified different issues as being important. Alexandra Kollontai, even Lenin's sister, were very important women in their time.

Are you now resurrecting this debate?

Carolina: Yes, but we don't want to develop our own theory from scratch. We see ourselves as Marxist-Leninists and at the same time we want to develop a sense of our own individuality. To give you an example. In 1988, at a three-day seminar for Cuban social scientists, an ideological debate developed out of one of Che Guevara's essays, '*El Hombre y el Socialismo*' ('Man/People and Socialism'). In it Che discusses the 'New Man'. We contrasted this with our own theses. First of all, we didn't like the term 'new man' but nevertheless we respect Che. The creation of the 'new man' comes about through the genesis of a new man and a new woman. We women don't want to be like men with all their negative characteristics, just as little as men should be like women with their negative characteristics. I'm talking about this whole psychological heritage of women based on a culture of oppression. No one should be like this classic subservient woman in the future.

At the Fifth Latin American and Caribbean Feminist Meeting in Argentina, lesbians are proposing a female role model which simply rejects men as providing any role model at all. Are lesbians a subject for discussion in the Federation? Are there any 'out' lesbians among you?

Alicia: Our organisation is very open and lesbians are a part of it. So, yes, there are 'out' lesbian members of the Federation.

There are a striking number of workshops at the feminist meeting on the issues of violence against women and sexuality. Are you Cubans affected by these issues?

Alicia: Yes, very much so. Violence against women is perhaps not as widespread in Cuba as in other countries but nevertheless it does exist, especially violence in marriage or a relationship.

HUMAN RIGHTS AND WOMEN'S RIGHTS

Rosalina Tuyuc (Guatemala)

From grief comes strength: indigenous women's resistance

After Colombia, the Central American republic of Guatemala has the most serious human rights abuses in the continent. Apart from trade unionists, student and political opposition groups, the victims of the army's systematic terror are primarily indigenous peasants and agricultural workers whom the forces of oppression accuse of being 'subversive' supporters of the armed resistance. These assumptions are based on their social position and ethnic identity.

Since the late 1970s approximately 50,000 Guatemalan women have lost their husbands through this state repression. There are no exact figures since many of the widows have fled from the war zones to be absorbed by the slums of the capital. On top of poverty, they often suffer social isolation, as the army refers to their dead husbands as having been 'subversive' or even maintains that they've 'gone underground' as guerrillas. In Guatemala it is perilous to have anything to do with subversives and their families.

In order to overcome this isolation and fight together for their rights and against repression, some of these women united in 1988 to form the National Association of Guatemalan Widows (CONAVIGUA). At first CONAVIGUA was not taken very seriously, as most of its members were indigenous women who could hardly speak Spanish or read and write. But this self-help organisation has now become respected not only in Guatemala but also internationally. Recent CONAVIGUA initiatives such as the exhumation of mass graves - memorials to the military massacres of the early 1980s - and a controversial campaign against military conscription, have propelled the organisation to the frontline of Guatemala's political struggle. Reason enough for Guatemala's rulers to threaten and persecute the women of CONAVIGUA. Rosalina Tuyuc is one of the founders of this unique human rights organisation which now has around 9,000 members.

* * * * * * * * * *

Why did you found CONAVIGUA? What were your aims?

We started off with small groups of widows back in 1985. They didn't only involve women who'd lost their husbands because of the repression, but also women whose husbands had died through illness. Some had just been abandoned by their husbands. Then, in 1986, Vinicio Cerezo came into power. He talked a lot about wanting to help the widows and orphans. For many women that was a great hope. They thought that with the power he had as president he could solve some of our problems. But the whole of 1987 went by without a single response to the the widows' groups' proposals. When 1988 also went by, we realised that women's pain was once more a subject of mirth for the government, even though most of us are widows because the military and the civil patrols abducted our husbands and murdered them. So we decided to convene the First National Meeting of Widows. It took place in September 1988 and it was there we elected a national leadership to steer our organisation. CONAVIGUA was born out of the great pain and harsh experiences which each one of us has experienced in Guatemala. That's what unites us, plus the hope for a better life for our children and our determination to gain the respect we deserve as widows. Those were the main reasons why we organised ourselves.

Initially the organisation grew quite quickly. Has the increased repression recently made it more difficult for women to participate? Are the women more afraid?

When we decided to found the organisation, there were about 200 of us in small groups dispersed throughout Quiché, Chimaltenango and Sololá. Today there are about 9,000 women. Yes, violence was a big hindrance for us. It left approximately 45,000 to 50,000 widows behind in Guatemala. Not to mention the rapes committed by soldiers in the provinces and all the pregnancies which resulted. From day one the organisation has been a target for a lot of persecution. Considering we've been at war for the past ten or twenty years, it's a miracle we've managed to create our organisation at all. But awareness is developing among the women that our only chance of defence is to be united, organised and to fight together.

Perhaps it's the first time in history that Guatemalan women have created their own organisation. We're the ones who make the decisions and analyse our problems. Lots of widows haven't yet joined the organisation. We want to unite a fair portion of them but that depends a great deal on the situation. Many can't take part because of the heavy militarisation in the provinces. Some have requested a visit from us but because of a lack of human and economic resources it's difficult for us to be active throughout the whole country. We've also started putting announcements on the radio about our cultural and religious activities which has helped us get in touch with a lot more widows.

Does that mean that, apart from the 9,000 members of CONAVIGUA, many more women support the organisation without officially being able to join it?

Yes, there are a lot of women who can't join because they're not allowed to, like some of our women who are living in the 'development zones' of the Ixil Triangle and can only leave their locality every three months. They give some of them permission for 24 hours, others for 36 hours. But on condition they say where they're going, how much money they're taking with them, what kind of clothes they're taking. And if they come back one hour late, they're threatened and have to pay a fine to get back into the village. But, inspite of that, the women are still prepared to come and get involved, if only out of pure necessity to fight for their most urgent needs, like food, health and their children's education.

Another problem is the military barracks in all the rural areas. Many widows have been warned by the military not to join our organisation on the grounds that CONAVIGUA is a guerrilla organisation. The military barge into houses and demand food at eleven, twelve or one o'clock at night. In the barracks too, they force women to do the washing and make tortillas. This is a constant problem for the women and they've had their fill of it so they come to our organisation in search of a forum for their struggles.

We get no support from the government because CONAVIGUA is an organisation of women who've largely been widowed as result of the army's repression. Instead of helping us, they slander us. They marginalise us because we're women, because we're indigenous women. We all know that we're not fighting against the military or trying to topple the government. Our aim is to get them to accept us as individuals, as people. Yes, they murdered our husbands, but there are laws to punish them. It's not up to us to take revenge. What we've publicly demanded is that the murderers reponsible for the massacres be punished according to the law.

Our present struggle has come from the hunger, misery and injustice we're suffering. In each of the provinces we see that most women no longer have enough to eat because the cost of survival is increasing every day. Let alone clothing, shoes and medicine. When there's nothing to eat, there's more illness, not only in women, but also in children. We've asked for economic support to be given directly to our organisation and human rights organisations, not to the government because it's received a lot of assistance in the name of widows, orphans, refugees and displaced people from the United Nations High Commissioner For Refugees (UNHCR) and other organisations. But who knows what's happened to this assistance? What I do know is that the repression has got worse, so we're asking for support to come directly to us and not via the government. Yes, corn and beans do get through. But the pittance they give us is just a few crumbs and even then only on condition that we acknowledge that our husbands were kidnapped and murdered by the guerrillas. We won't accept that.

What's your relationship like with other popular movements? Is there cooperation?

Each organisation has its own demands but all popular movements support unity and solidarity. We're all part of the UASP, the biggest association of trade unions and popular organisations founded in 1988. For us the UASP is the voice of all our people. Right from the start, CONAVIGUA has supported the demands of the trade unions as well as the students, the working people and the agricultural workers, the CUC, the GAM and the CERJ. Until now the situation has almost always divided us. The more divided we are, the better for the government, because then no one can exert pressure on them. So the solution for the popular movement has always been the promotion of unity and greater harmony with the political parties, the Church and the cooperatives. But our steps towards unity have provoked yet more threats from the military. The UASP was accused of being a guerrilla organisation and possessing a large arsenal of weapons.

Can you tell me a bit about the specific difficulties which the women face - in their contacts with other organisations, with men and their families?

Few of us widows have any permanent work. And when we do get a job it's on the coffee, sugar and cotton plantations. The women who work there earn nothing more than their food and they have to take their children with them. A large proportion of our members go to the plantations, year after year. It's so badly paid there that it's not enough even to send your child to school. Apart from this, most women make handicrafts for a living. But the people who profit the most from these are the middlemen who only pay a pittance for the work. The problem is that women's work is so undervalued.

Our experience of struggle has taught us something, because at first the men reckoned we women couldn't achieve anything. There's always been this *machismo* and its basic principle is that only men can speak, only men can participate and women must simply obey. When a baby is born, their response is: 'It's a girl, she can't go to school.' Later when you get married, they say: 'now you're the property of your husband.' In church they say the same thing to you, you have to accept it. And so women have always been dominated, they weren't allowed to speak for themselves. When we women organised ourselves, many people reacted in exactly the same way. Some men thought: 'These poor women! We didn't get anywhere and now they're falling into the same trap. They can't read or write, they can't even speak Spanish.' But when they saw how our organisation developed, they had to change their tune. To give you an example, we were once given some fertiliser which we loaded and unloaded from the trucks ourselves. Incidents like that made the men realise that even women are capable of such things.

These days a lot of men actually encourage their wives to support CONAVIGUA and participate in our courses. Until now our organisation hasn't addressed the needs of married women, but there are hundreds of them who've asked us to work with them and want to join our courses. The courses are based on our own experience, and our way of life. Not the way the government programme does it. Take their health programme: what are we told in it? 'If you want to keep healthy, eat eggs and meat every day and drink milk.' But that's impossible for our women because they haven't got the money to buy that kind of food.

We've been given quite a lot of support by the popular movement. There are women intellectuals, doctors, teachers and lawyers in these organisations but they don't look down on us because the amount of respect each individual commands depends on his or her personal contribution. A woman has to earn respect through her work and her moral behaviour in exactly the same way as a man has to.

One of our most important experiences was our participation in the National Dialogue along with a lot of intellectuals.[1] We have no secondary schooling but despite that our organisation has been respected. All our representatives have a seat on the executive of the various commissions conducting the National Dialogue. We're treated with respect because of our painful experiences - something of a novelty for us. Living under a military regime, we're repressed politically, economically, militarily and socially. The state rules over men, men rule over women, and women over their children. And when you don't give children what they want, they sometimes beat the animals, the cat or the dog. There's a pecking order from top to bottom. We've got to change this way of behaving inflicted upon us. Our struggle is not directed against men because men have also suffered. We'll always fight alongside the men.

Footnotes

[1] The National Dialogue was initiated by President Cerezo in the late 1980s to try and reach a consensus with Guatemalan civil society as to what changes were needed in the country.

Rosario Ibarra (Mexico)

The search for disappeared sons: how it changed the mothers

During the 1970s and 1980s serious human rights abuses were a cruel reality in the many Latin American countries ruled by military dictatorships. Disappearances signified a new type of repression: people were dragged away from their jobs or homes or simply hauled into cars on the street and never seen again. The authorities claimed not to have any information regarding the fate of the disappeared. Anxious families or girlfriends frequently had to put up with cynical official explanations: perhaps they had gone travelling or been the victims of violent crime.

Refusing to come to terms with the disappearance of their children and partners, the relatives - predominantly women - began to unite in many Latin American countries, not only to find solace and support from each other but also to demand an explanation. 'We lost them alive, we want them back alive' was the slogan of the Mothers of the Plaza de Mayo in Argentina, whose weekly silent protest march became an international symbol of the struggle against human rights abuses and state terror.

Disappearances have not been confined to countries ruled by military dictatorships; they are also a phenomenon in civilian Mexico with its formally democratic government. Fifteen years ago Jesús, Rosario Ibarra's son, was carried off in Northern Mexico, never to be seen again. Since then Rosario, as president of the Committee for the Defence of Prisoners, the Persecuted and the Disappeared, has been fighting not only for her son, but for all political prisoners and disappeared people in Mexico.

Rosario Ibarra was the first female candidate for the Mexican presidency in 1982. As an independent candidate, nominated by the Revolutionary Workers' Party (PRT), she only received 2.5% of the votes. In 1989 she was nominated for the third time for the Nobel peace prize. In the following interview Rosario talks about her political struggle and her specific development as a woman which she has undergone with other mothers.

* * * * * * * * * *

Rosario, are there many disappeared people and political prisoners in Mexico?

We have a list of 522 disappeared people but in reality there are more than that. Through public and international support and action by Amnesty International and other worldwide human rights organisations, we've been able to free 148 disappeared people until now.

When was the worst time?

It was particularly hard when there was no organisation to fight for the disappeared. In 1972 and 1973 people began to disappear systematically. At that time some of the groups fighting for democracy took up arms when the government flatly refused to have any dialogue with them. The number of disappearances started to increase just as this armed resistance began to get organised. That's when the families of the disappeared began to unite. We came across each other in government offices where we were demanding the release of our children. We were all mothers, filing in one after the other. In the end we decided to found an organisation called Eureka.

When people disappear or are arrested for political reasons, is it reported directly to Eureka?

When someone disappears, we're usually contacted directly, because - sad as it may sound - we're 'specialists' in this area. We always start with the official legal channels, as we're obliged to do, because the Mexican government often complains to the UN or to Amnesty International that we don't follow the correct legal procedures. We can only tell the UN that the government is making a mockery of the whole thing: it tells them there can't be any disappeared people in Mexico because there's an institution, LOCATEL, (a sort of telephonic information bureau run by the Red Cross), which registers all people who temporarily cannot be located (for example, after an accident). But LOCATEL didn't exist at the time when our children disappeared and, anyway, there's no access to information about secret prisons like, for example, the famous *Campo Militar No. 1.*

To get back to our procedures, we go to the public prosecutor's office and if nothing can be found out that way, the whole thing gets referred to the chief constable. If nothing comes of that or we're deliberately put off the scent, then we know it's a political case and the Ministry of the Interior must be called to testify. Our last resort is to turn to international institutions like Amnesty or the UN and organise letter and phone campaigns to pressurise the government. As a last ditch attempt, we hold demonstrations and meetings in front of the national palace where the government sits.

That's how we've waged our struggle for the past 14 years.

Your son disappeared 15 years ago. How has this changed your life?

The changes to me happened quite gradually as I got more involved in the issue. I've certainly got a more radical attitude towards a system that takes away our sons and daughters and our men and women. I've realised that the metamorphosis inside me also happened to many other mothers in my position. I've often said that we were larvae at the beginning. Then we slipped out as butterflies, moved our wings and flew off in all directions. As we searched for our children, we got this defiant urge for freedom, for the freedom to simply look for our children. You see, many of us didn't have this 'freedom' because of our husbands' domination.

It's sad but many fathers forbade their wives from going out on the streets to look for their children. There were some who had to choose between looking for their children and staying at home with their husbands. It's terrible, this old male chauvinism!

But, despite this, many of us older women were stirred to fight. Something wonderful came out of this. You could tell that women had changed in relation to their surroundings because normally children's education is their responsibility and in the end they're the ones who determine their children's characters, including the gender type-casting: 'you're a boy, so you must be such and such, and you're a girl, so you have to behave like this...'

Through the search for their children, the mothers began to question their way of looking at things and to understand their children's protests, even their daughters'. So they're now calling for the defence of the rights of *everyone*, including women's rights. Yes, I think this has been a valuable change.

Through the search for their children, have the mothers acquired a more comprehensive political awareness?

At first the women said, 'my son was good, they carried him off because he was mixing with a bad lot.' They didn't understand the basic reasons why their sons had got involved in the struggle, but gradually it dawned on them: 'if my son was a good person, then what he did must also have been good.' So they came to the conclusion that social and political struggles for the rights of workers and peasants to health, housing and education were all right. Very soon they came to regard their own personal struggle as a component of this social struggle. 'I'm going out to fight,' they said, 'so that when my kid comes home, we can go on fighting together.' These days they don't say: 'when my kid comes home, I can go home again.' Instead they say, 'we're going to carry on together, because we've lost a lot of time.'

As a result of this, are these women taking to the streets to demand other things?

Yes. It's not our first priority, but we do attend various women's meetings and congresses. All the women's groups give us a lot of support. Many of the older women in our organisation, who were brought up in a more old-fashioned way, are now starting to question things like they would never have dreamt of before.

Are you still hopeful that even those who disappeared a long time ago might still reappear?

Yes, we are, and that's not just wishful thinking. Some people who disappeared for nine or ten years were discovered in secret prisons - even after eleven years - so why shouldn't people who disappeared twelve, thirteen or even fourteen years ago still be alive? Unless of course they were murdered in cold blood or have died from illness or malnutrition. But we want them back alive. We've just started a big campaign again and recently managed to talk to the president about our action for this year. Maybe we'll get some people released.

Chabela (Vicenta) Camusso (Uruguay)

Black women in a white world: the search for a new identity

Uruguay is regarded as one of the most European republics in Latin America, its dominant culture having been shaped by European immigrants. There is little recognition of the fact that Uruguay also has African roots; between four and five per cent of Uruguayans have African ancestry, following the transportation of black men and women to Latin America and the Caribbean as slaves to work on white people's plantations. For centuries their way of life, their culture and their resistance has either been absent from historical texts or distorted by romanticism. No one ever asked black Uruguayans about their own conception of themselves. On the whole, blacks have only been important to the rulers of Uruguay during election campaigns. Their promises of improvement to the blacks' miserable living conditions have been offered simply to win votes. *'Al negro dale vino y tambor'* ('give a black wine and drums'), goes the popular saying in Montevideo.

Vicenta Camusso - or 'Chabela', as she is called - is a representative of a black women's group. She talks about the problems facing the majority of Afro-Uruguayan women who, long after the abolition of slavery, still remain in the poorest sectors of Uruguayan society. As well as projects aimed at the improvement of black women's living conditions, the women from the women's group of the black organisation *Mundo Afro* are trying to develop their own political identity as black women. In 'Chabela's' view, this is a process which requires an independent organisation and thus a certain distance from existing (white) women's groups.

* * * * * * * * * *

As a black women in Uruguay, why do you feel the need to organise?

For lots of reasons; firstly, because we belong to the lowest social class; secondly, because black women are discriminated against in Uruguay, and in fact doubly discriminated against; as women and as blacks. Racism in

Uruguay is not as obvious as in many other countries but it exists everywhere. We women need to organise so as to develop as human beings - quite simply, to grow. It's important to stand by the colour of our skins and to see our ethnic roots as something positive. This society's racism has encouraged us to betray the colour of our own skin. Many black women would prefer to be white; we're conditioned to think white is better and that means losing our common heritage and our ethnic community.

When did you join the black women's organisation?

I joined it shortly after it was founded towards the end of 1989. It didn't come out of the blue; it developed out of *Mundo Afro* (Afro World), a mixed-sex black organisation in which there'd always been a women's group. But this group mainly did social work without any reference to ethnic identity. Then when the black women's group was founded with an emphasis on *women's* work, I joined for personal reasons. For years on end I've been trying to find a niche for myself among white people. In the process I've put myself under a great deal of pressure and suppressed a lot of things about my personality. So first of all it was really important for me to talk over these problems with the other women in the group. We give ourselves specific goals now in our efforts to develop a different relationship with white people.

So are you a sort of consciousness-raising group?

No, talking is just part of it. For example, we're currently planning to set up outpatients' clinics for women, mainly offering gynaecological and psychological treatment.

Only for black women?

Yes, in theory. Obviously we wouldn't close the door on white women but our target group is primarily black women. We're also planning to open a legal advice centre, mainly concentrating on employment law so that black women get to know their rights. The majority have had a very poor education. Most of them only go to primary school and leave after six years. Many of them tend to trust their white employers implicitly, even when he withholds things from them. Either that or they don't dare contradict him because they're used to being treated as ignorant in this world where white people are considered superior. Another part of our legal work is prostitutes' rights. There's a high percentage of prostitutes in the black population and we're trying to organise them. We're also trying to help black women prisoners. Considering that black women represent only 4.5

percent of the Uruguayan population, a very high percentage of them are in prison.

We're also planning to set up a research centre, a sort of data bank to enable us to give a more systematic answer to some of our questions. And while I'm on the subject of our future plans, we intend to set up some small businesses. We've already had some experience of this. In one workshop, for example, black women make sportswear for children. They buy the cloth at a cooperative and the sewing machines and other equipment comes from a white women's organisation. Some women sew and others deal with the sales. In this way we're creating jobs which liberate black women from the kind of traditional jobs open to them like domestic service. Smallscale workshops are ideal for raising black women's consciousness.

You seem to have a lot of plans. How big is your organisation then?

Well, all these ideas came from a group of twenty women. Five of them have a lot of time on their hands at the moment because they're unemployed.

So do they have any income?

No, of course not. They live with their parents and manage somehow... The rest of us divide up the work according to our interests and areas of expertise. For example, I study law so I'm particularly involved in legal issues. Other women are textile workers or dressmakers, so they're involved in setting up the small businesses. Some work with prostitutes. Don't go away thinking we're moving mountains. On the contrary, it's all happening at a snail's pace. The most practical thing we have is the little sewing business.

Why don't you fight racism alongside men?

We do! Because we're both. Women *and* blacks, and most of us are also members of mixed, black organisations. For example, I'm a member of *Mundo Afro* and work there with men. Our group sees itself as a sort of new women's committee of *Mundo Afro* but with autonomous decision-making powers. That means we determine our own programme of work without losing sight of *Mundo Afro's* general direction.

Do you see yourselves as feminists?

Speaking for the group as a whole, I'd tend to say no. You know how it is. Your upbringing and the things you hear in the street - they make women shy away from this word. Many of us would definitely describe ourselves as feminists. I'd even say the others are feminists in their behaviour and their work. But we don't want to offend anyone so we're a bit cautious and try to show what a good thing feminism is by example. Let's hope we can convince people.

What are relations like between you black women and the black men in Mundo Afro? You just mentioned autonomous decision-making powers. Are the men interested in your work?

I think we've achieved more than the men. It may be a slow process, as I just said, but once we've got something into our heads we do actually carry it through. Even if it sometimes means losing a night's sleep over it. The men are curious about us: 'let's see what these black women are up to,' they say.

Do they try to get involved?

No, but they tell us what they think. For example, they don't want us to be pushed about by the white women's groups. That would seem to them like a defeat for blacks as a whole.

Is this how it usually is between black men and women? Do the men feel responsible for the women?

No, not at all. Black families traditionally revolve around the women. It's not organised in a patriarchal way. The women look after the children, have jobs and generally get out and about. Obviously the men also go to work, but the burden of responsibility for the family is carried by the women. So if there's something to fight for, then it tends to be the women who band together.

If that's the case, why have you taken so long to organise as black women?

(She laughs)... It's probably got something to do with our view of ourselves. We take to the streets when there's something immediate to fight for but when the entire white world around us keeps telling us we're second-class citizens, we start to believe it and we sometimes think we're not worthy enough to have our own space.

In Europe both black and white feminists can be accused of being racist. Do you have similar experiences in Uruguay?

Sometimes white women's groups don't understand why we want to organise separately as black women and criticise us for making women more divided. I think they'd prefer it if we joined the existing women's groups. I wouldn't go so far as to say there's *always* latent racism there, although we do come across the odd racist comment from time to time. We're not trying to provoke white women. We're more interested in coming to terms with ourselves as black women and getting rid of our shame. We have to deal with that among ourselves first. A white woman can't really understand what it's like, except at an intellectual level. She has no experience of what it means to be treated with contempt everywhere you go, as nothing more than a sex object.

Do you see any fundamental differences between life for blacks in the country and in the towns?

Oh yes, there's a very big difference. For a start, black women in the country are not organised.

Does your women's group only operate in Montevideo?

We've put out feelers into the interior and made some visits there. But any organisation's work is difficult there because people are very isolated. Some black women there are involved in white women's groups. The problem is that in many regions black women work as live-in maids in exactly the same way as their mothers did and their grandmothers before them. Many are illiterate and have absolutely no idea how the world has changed.

In the past, the black population of Montevideo was largely concentrated in one district. For this reason along there was strong community feeling. What's happened to it?

The 'black district' has existed for forty years now. It started from two so-called *conventillos* in Montevideo which are large houses built around a courtyard, with each room occupied by a different family. It was there that the lives of the black people in Montevideo unfolded. As time went by, many families rented or bought a little house round about, but they always stayed in the district.

During the dictatorship these *conventillos* disappeared. One of them, called *Medio Mundo* (Half World) on the coast was completely demolished. The occupants who had been born and had grown up and spent their whole lives there were rehoused far away in a hilly part of the town in little boxes - cheap, pre-fabricated houses without bathrooms. So the dictatorship got what it wanted. Today the blacks lead scattered lives and the traditional, neighbourly relationships of the past have gone.

Do Uruguay's political parties take much notice of black people?

No, they're not interested in black women's concerns or blacks in general. For them, racism is not an issue. As a left-wing activist, I must admit this is also true of the Left. And it's always been that way. The lives of blacks and whites have always developed on completely different planes. Even in the *Tupamaros* the guerrillas, there are only three or four blacks and only one black woman, to my knowledge.

Perhaps international political pressure could help. Black women's groups have now been formed in several Latin American countries. Do you have any contact with them?

We tend to find that our own situation is completely different from other people's elsewhere. To my knowledge, there were some attempts to get women together at the Fifth Feminist Meeting in Argentina. Otherwise I only remember one joint meeting between blacks from Porto Alegre in Brazil and blacks from Uruguay in Montevideo in May 1990. It was a mixed meeting which set up a women's commission.

What do you see as the main differences between the situation of blacks in different countries?

Firstly I'd draw a dividing line between those of us in Latin America and those of us in the Caribbean. In the Caribbean the number of blacks is far higher so they're not exposed to so much racism. But the economic situation there is also completely different. With the exception of some parts of Brazil which has the most experience of black movements, we Latin Americans live in a white world. At the Argentinian meeting it was obvious that we needed some sort of network so a commission of women from Brazil, Uruguay, Jamaica, the Dominican Republic and Haiti was created. Basically their task will be to organise a meeting of Latin American and Caribbean black women, though where and when it will take place is not clear yet.[1]

Footnotes

[1] The meeting took place from 19 to 25 July, 1992, in Santo Domingo, Dominican Republic.

Lady[1] Elizabeth Repetto (Uruguay)

Women against violence against women

Male violence against women - whether physical, mental, sexual or economic - is a key issue for women in Latin America. In numerous countries there are now initiatives offering practical help or attempting to put a stop to rapists and wrongdoers, often husbands, through publicity campaigns and proposals for constitutional amendments. Police stations staffed by women in Brazil, Peru and Uruguay, are just one innovation enabling women to at least report offences to female members of the police. In Montevideo, a relatively peaceful city compared to São Paulo or Mexico City, over thirty women died in 1991 alone as a result of sexual violence. Every day nine women lose their hearing, suffer detached retinas, broken bones or other serious injuries. Ten receive death threats, three are raped and six come away with superficial injuries. Only two per cent of the reported attackers are sentenced. Some sixty women - a small proportion of the real number of women affected - seek advice every month from the offices of *SOS Mujer* in the centre of Montevideo. Lady Elizabeth Repetto, director of this sanctuary, talks about the horrors of everyday male violence and explores its causes.

* * * * * * * * * *

When I read the name of your centre, SOS Mujer, *over the entrance, I was reminded of women's refuges and emergency numbers with the same name in Europe, that work with battered women like you do. Is* SOS Mujer *founded in cooperation with feminists abroad?*

No, not at all. Quite the opposite, in fact, because the name comes directly from the Spanish language and from our experiences here. *SOS Mujer* is a pun: on the one hand it means the well-known emergency S.O.S.; on the other hand, '*sos*' comes from the verb '*ser*' ('to be') which in Uruguayan

Spanish means 'you are'. So *SOS Mujer* also means 'you are a woman, be self-aware!' It's very important for battered women with little self-respect to grasp this. Our key task here at the centre is to try and instill self-awareness in the women. When a woman comes here and explains her problems, she's obviously suffering from the beatings but she also feels guilty and worried about her children and even her husband; should she report him or get a divorce? Then he'd be alone without domestic support. What would become of him and his work? She always sees herself as the very last person to worry about. Women don't dare think about themselves at all. We tell them: 'You know, there are solutions and ways out. Above all, you yourself have a right to be happy. No one has the right to beat you or to hurt you.' But this unsettles the women. They stress that they're really not complaining and they're doing all right, that it's a question of protecting the happiness of the children. They don't recognise that it's important they should be happy in themselves. So I ask: 'When did you last look in the mirror? When did you last wear make-up?' and I sense confusion in the women: what kind of a question is that? A woman doesn't have a right to that sort of thing. Even when she is sick, her husband comes and drags her out of bed to make him a meal.

How do women pluck up the courage to come to SOS Mujer?

Well, word's got around that this centre exists. But clearly to come here is a giant step. Few women manage this step on their own, maybe none completely on their own. The more avenues of help, the better. In general they're sent by a doctor, or by a neighbour, a social worker in a hospital, or they've heard about *SOS Mujer* on the radio. We don't make any visits ourselves because when we did go into hospital or visit women at home, we realised that after that the women didn't dare take the step of coming to us. The fact that a woman actually comes into the centre shows that she at least wants to get out of her current situation.

I'd like to say something else to you about the term, 'battered woman'. In our opinion 'battered' isn't only related to physical blows. Battered women may have suffered all possible kinds of violence: mental, sexual and, strange as it may sound, economic violence. As the economic situation is very difficult in this country, men's violence against women is often expressed through money. A woman with five children, for example, is in no position to work outside the home because she's got nowhere to take the children. This woman is regarded as unemployed. Housework, washing, cooking, ironing, looking after the children, taking them to school, aren't considered as 'work'. So the only one who 'works' in the family is the husband. As a result he thinks he's the only one who has rights and gives her 1,000 pesos to look after the children when she really needs at least

10,000 pesos. That's violence, because the woman has to buy things on credit, borrow money elsewhere, or even skip meals. And as she doesn't earn any money herself, she can't buy herself any shoes or clothes, she can't go to the hairdresser's. She's the maid in her own home, so to speak, without any rights of her own. That's very very common. There are women who don't know how much their husbands earn. They haven't the slightest idea because they've never caught sight of one of his pay slips. If that's not violence...

When was SOS Mujer *founded?*

We've been working since 1987 and were making plans and inquiries a year before that. We started off working with prostitutes who'd noticed how much their everyday life was affected by violence. The violence which came on the one hand from the men who sought their services and demanded God knows what from them, and on the other, from the pimps who stripped the money from their pockets. And then on top of that there was the violence they had to endure from the police. In our group we had a clear understanding of the violence prostitutes are exposed to, but we also began to realise that basically every woman can be exposed to this form of violence. We had a lot of discussions, made inquiries, visited hospitals. It quickly became clear that the problem was far more serious than we'd previously thought. And what was equally serious was that there wasn't a single institution in the whole country that worked with battered women or was concerned with the issue of violence against women. As a result of this, those directly affected organised themselves and founded the *Asociación de Meretrices Públicas Uruguayas* (Uruguayan Prostitute's Association), a sort of union. And we also started a working group focus on the issue of violence against women in general. We then got the chance to attend a series of lectures, given by people from the university of Buenos Aires which were sponsored by the Ministry of Public Culture and Education. We made contact with them and went to Buenos Aires and Mar del Plata to attend a meeting of forty women's refuges. In Argentina they've had more experience of working in this area. Since Argentina and Uruguay are very similar when it comes to violence, we were able to adopt the same structure as they have, with individual advice for women, self-help groups, work with the children of battered wives, for our own work here.

So that's how *SOS Mujer* was founded. When we first set it up we had no idea what we'd taken on. Some days we advise as many as six or seven women. And we know very well they're only the tip of the iceberg. In November 1989, a woman who'd come to us for advice and help was murdered on the corner here. The attacker was her husband. The woman, Flor, lived here in this house. I must add, of course, that our centre here isn't a women's refuge.

It isn't a refuge?

No, normally the women don't live here. Flor came from the interior and didn't know where to stay. She also had three little children with her. We'd only just bought the house and we let her have a room until she could see her way more clearly, had found a job and could then rent a flat. The woman filed for divorce. Unfortunately, the female solicitor we'd hired was forced by the judge to supply Flor's actual address on one of the summonses. After that the husband surfaced here from time to time to threaten her. He wound us all up by ringing the bell incessantly and hammering on the door and trying to take the children. He told me his wife belonged to him and no one else and he'd murder her. On 12 November 1989, a Sunday morning, Flor left the house to buy some bread in the shop opposite. He lay in wait for her and stabbed her. Cases like Flor's affect us very deeply. After all, she lived here with us; we'd built up a close relationship with her. Obviously we know that Flor is in no way a special case. Ten days after Flor's murder another woman, Isabel Daluz, was stabbed by her husband in front of twelve policemen in a police station in one of the outlying districts. Flor was certainly someone special to us because we knew her, but she's by no means the exception. We feel the same pain and grief for Flor as we do any woman who suffers a violent death.

What normally happens when a woman comes to you?

First we have preliminary interviews where we try to shed some light on her specific problems from as many viewpoints as possible. Some aspects are common to almost all cases. For example, in 95 per cent of cases the wife beater is the son of a wife beater. In other words, these men have already internalised beating as a form of expression. There's actually a typical profile of a wife beater. From the outside he's a thoroughly nice man; he's a good neighbour, a good work colleague, an excellent friend, a friendly, lovable person with charming manners. But he's barely in the door before he starts harassing his wife. The only person he beats is his wife. We try to find out more details, such as whether there's any alcoholism involved. There are lots of assumptions made about this. Many people believe a man beats his wife because he's an alcoholic. That's not true. A man beats his wife because he's a violent person. Alcohol can be a trigger. But just look at how many alcoholics aren't wife beaters and how many wife beaters aren't alcoholics. We hear of many wife beaters who are thought of as nice chaps. Neighbours say he was always on his best behaviour, always ready to help at any given moment. Even the solicitors describe their clients like that.

Recently we hired a female solicitor for a woman who came to our centre.

This solicitor was completely stunned. She had absolutely no idea what we were talking about. She neither knew that our institution existed nor that violence against women existed. 'What worries me,' she said, 'is that the husband is such an exceptional person, so sweet-tempered, so gentle, so friendly...' We showed her the documents we'd compiled against him. This was a man who was a wife beater and he came from a family in which there are other wife beaters. He was extremely aggressive. The solicitor's eyes grew rounder and rounder. She couldn't believe that the man who'd visited her and convinced her of his harmlessness and his exceptionally big heart was the same man we were discussing. This type of man can surprise even the likes of us, in spite of our experience. Flor's husband, for example, always came in a suit and tie. He looked like Alain Delon. Yet he's a typical wife beater. Outside the home he's an exceptionally nice person and beats his wife behind closed doors. If you ask him about it, he evades the issue and talks about the money problems which are worrying him and making him nervy and moans about not earning enough. But of course that's no excuse because if he's not earning enough, then why doesn't he beat his boss? Or if he's out of work why doesn't he lie in wait for the president and chop his head off when he leaves his residence? But no one does that. Instead, the men go home and beat their wives. In private they seek out a physically weaker, submissive being who they regard as their possession. I'd like to know whether you have similar experiences in Europe.

Definitely. Most rapes are perpetrated by male members of the family or relatives. The scene of the crime is hardly ever a dark alley but the victim's own home or a friend's home. It's difficult for women to denounce rapist from their own family or among their friends.

It's exactly the same here. We don't have any statistics but one thing that's really astonished us is the social background of wife beaters. Beating women is by no means confined to the slums, as some would like to believe. Wife beaters exist in every social class. The higher the class, the more refined the violence. We've had the wives of men here who have a very high profile in society, the wives of politicians and also businessmen - and sometimes they themselves are well known to the public because of their own profession.

What happens after the preliminary interview?

It doesn't stop at one interview. The *SOS* worker who held the initial conversation continues to see the woman once a week or once a fortnight. Parallel to that she encourages the woman to join in a self-help group. That's our most important service because through the groups the women discover that they're not alone and that other women have similar experiences. Through conversations and advice the women begin to help each other. Some want to take courses in handicrafts to make ends meet. We can also offer legal advice through a solicitor who works with us. If women want to instigate proceedings against their husbands with her help, then it's almost free. This solicitor is an exception. In their training here solicitors aren't usually prepared for the issue of 'violence against women' at all. At the university of Buenos Aires there's an additional training course for law students on violence in the family. For the coming academic year we've made arrangements with the people from Buenos Aires for the introduction of a two-year course here at the university of Montevideo.

Very few people in Uruguay who meet battered wives in the course of their professional work - solicitors, doctors, psychiatrists, psychologists, sociologists - have any real grasp of the problem. They look down on the women. So we've come to the conclusion that the preliminary interviews with women who've come to us shouldn't be conducted by these experts, as we initially thought. It turned out to be much better when a woman from our own group offered her services instead. The very first thing the women need is an atmosphere of sympathy and warmth. First of all, everything that's oppressed the woman has to come out in the open without some analytical brain immediately sifting and ordering it all. They simply need someone to listen, believe them and give them sympathy. The experts haven't been prepared for that in their training. From our past experiences we realised there were a lot of women who got stuck along the way and who didn't come here anymore because they weren't able to build up a relationship with the person who'd first advised them.

How many women work at your centre?

There are five of us. Then there's a solicitor and also a psychiatrist who works with us on some cases because many women are really ill after twenty, thirty years of abuse. Of course we try and work with the healthy side a woman may still possess, but she also needs someone to attend to her sick side.

Is the psychiatrist a man? Do you also work with men?

Yes, he's a man. We're not afraid of contact with men, quite the reverse. The women shouldn't get the impression that all men are bad, or that they're all violent and useless. That's why they also need a positive counter-image.

Isn't there a danger they'll think they've also been mistaken about their own husbands?

That hasn't happened to us yet. At least I haven't heard of such a case. Being in a couple is also something very beautiful. And if you've had one bad experience with a relationship, it doesn't mean it always has to turn out badly or that all men are the same. I'm convinced of that at least, otherwise I wouldn't have a boyfriend myself or I'd live with another woman. Besides, you also have to bear in mind that many men have now become more sensitive to the issue. Sometimes odd things happen to me. For example, when I go to the radio station to do a phone-in programme, it's mainly men who phone and they don't just call to make jokes or be rude. Admittedly that does happen, but they also ring to make serious suggestions or show their support. So not all men are bad or violent, though maybe most are.

Do you think official figures for abuse accurately reflect reality?

No, we reckon they only represent ten per cent of actual cases. Women don't usually file a report and if they end up in hospital they don't say exactly how they got hurt. They tend to go straight back to their old environment. And it seems that the police stations don't keep records on the number of reports. They are only registered at the one station staffed by women which is in Montevideo.

Isn't it a major step forward to have a police station staffed by women?

No, we're really not very happy about it. Firstly, there's only the one station which is right in the city centre and so it's only used by a very small number of women. Most incidents occur in the outlying districts and late at night or at the weekend when the station is closed. It was set up about three years ago. I don't know much about its background but the decision to have it was certainly not a particularly democratic one. CONAMU (National Women's Council), the women's group of the right-wing *Colorado* Party, which was the ruling party until the last elections, managed to persuade the minister for the interior to support their initiative. Those of us who've been involved with the issue of violence against women for four or five years now don't believe a station like that is much use. In Flor's case I phoned the station myself to ask for special protection for our house after Flor's husband had threatened to murder her and was hanging around the vicinity. They refused. They only take action once something's happened. In other words, Flor had to die before the police deigned to get involved. What use is that? What's more, the women police officers at the station haven't been trained at all for their special task. They're just policewomen who work there and during the dictatorship some of them tortured and body-searched women whose husbands had been arrested.

*Do you have any suggestions as to how this police station might be changed
or what alternatives there might be?*

In our experience there have to be people at every police station who've
been specially trained to deal with abused women in the appropriate manner.
If it's policewomen, all the better, but I wouldn't rule out men.

What's Uruguayan legislation like in this regard?

The legislation has a lot of shortcomings. For example, violence against
women is not a legal concept. In other words, it's not a crime to hit a woman.
So you always have to get round it by using related punishable offences.
Family judges, some of whom are now women, have recently become more
sensitive to the issue, but they still leave a great deal to be desired. One
thing we've learnt is that there's no solidarity among women. We women
don't simply feel solidarity towards each other just like that. A female
judge doesn't feel sympathetic *per se* towards a battered wife. It's just the
same with a female solicitor. She may even defend a wife beater at the
expense of his wife. We're simply victims of an upbringing which prevents
solidarity. I don't know if that's the case in all countries. Groups like ours
which work with women are still a relatively new concept here. We've
realised we often have problems when we try to work together that men
don't have. It's clear that group work is better with men than with women.
I think it's got something to do with upbringing. The little boy goes outside
to play ball with his friends and lets others have a go too; when a little girl
wants to go outside with her doll, her mother gives her strict instructions
not to let it out of her hands and not to let anyone take it away from her. So
we women are certainly more self-centred. In the Spanish-speaking world
we're always called 'queen', 'queen of the home', 'queen of the kitchen, of
washing, ironing', whatever's relevant. When we turn to less conventional
tasks, we lack the ability for solidarity, tolerance and understanding. We
still have a lot to learn in this respect. Incidentally, we aren't the only ones
to have these problems. You'll find it's the same for all women's groups.
That's why they're just as unstable as us. We women still have to learn to
socialise with one another and develop a sense of solidarity between us.

*In Europe there was this myth in the early days of the women's movement
that all women were equal, in solidarity with each other and united in
their aims. It still rankles today to have to admit that there's just as much
of a tendency towards hierarchies in women's groups as in any mixed group.
What's more, I think that these hierarchies, and those who submit to them,
are actually the stabilising factor in men's groups, and not solidarity. We
women are in the process of learning that we are different, that not all*

women have to get on well with all women. That creates dishonesty followed by frustration. But to change the subject: there's been a left-wing city council in Montevideo since March 1990. Does that make your work easier?

It's too soon to see any real results. Mind you, we haven't yet approached the city council with any solid proposal. We're thinking of suggesting they set up a women's refuge. At the moment there's a draft bill waiting for approval in parliament, which will oblige the government to take direct measures against violence towards women if it's passed. We want to wait and see the results of the vote. At first we intended to set up a women's refuge ourselves here, but in view of the economic situation in Uruguay, that would be impossible because it would inevitably turn into a permanent asylum since the women wouldn't have any opportunities to find work or pay for their own accommodation. Our centre couldn't afford that financially.

How has SOS Mujer *coped so far?*

Our centre is supported by 'Bread for the World' in Germany. At the moment we're completely dependent on this support. Really, we ought to write more project proposals but we haven't got the time. For example, I'm the leader of *SOS Mujer* but I still have to help with cleaning the toilets, draining the house when it's rained or cleaning the *mate* gourds. I also accompany women to the police station and go to international congresses and so on. I also have another job as a radio announcer and lastly, I'm a housewife.

What effect has the economic crisis of the past few years had on violence against women?

We thought you'd somehow got more of a grip on the problem in the industrialised countries. But when for example, we talk to visitors from Sweden we realise the problem there is exactly the same and that the only difference is that there's a better infrastructure in Sweden for women to use. So the crisis has exacerbated the lack of amenities rather than increased the actual number of acts of violence. Medical and psychological care is completely inadequate. Time and time again we're asked; what actually happens to the offenders? There's certainly not a single institution here which treats these men either psychologically or in any other way. In other countries, in Argentina, for example, there's experience in this kind of work and a good track record in things like self-help groups. We've heard that in Sweden men are given a prison sentence with psychiatric care, but when they come out of prison they go on beating their wives just as before. We know the cycle of violence is difficult to break; from mounting aggression, verbal attacks and finally physical blows, to promises never to hit her again, followed by renewed aggression. The only solution is separation. Naturally we don't directly advise the women to separate from their husbands, they have to come to this decision on their own. But often the women think they should stay with their husbands because of the children, whereas they're damaging the children by staying. They're presenting them with a behavioural model which will encourage their sons to become wife beaters themselves in the future and their daughters battered wives.

How did you get involved in this work yourself?

It was a series of coincidences. I was working as a secretary at the headquarters of one of the fishery cooperatives right here in this neighbourhood. We started working with prostitutes around here and *SOS Mujer* grew out of that. One day a novice priest who worked with me asked me if I could get hold of material about prostitutes while on a trip to Buenos Aires, so that we could set up a support organisation here as well. I did as he asked, although I got funny looks whenever I asked for information. In the process I met groups in Buenos Aires working on the issue of violence against women. That whetted my own interest, and I've been involved ever since *SOS Mujer* was founded.

Do you ever get new recruits who want to work here?

Yes, we get a lot of calls and a lot of women drop in and ask if they can help. At the moment we're in the process of setting up an induction programme. But not every woman can cope with this type of work because it's very upsetting and often in the middle of conversations your own personal experiences may suddenly emerge.

Do you have any supervision?

No, group members frequently meet to work through our own experiences. That's our own form of therapy.

What does your working day look like?

There are two shifts of four hours each. For example, I'm here in the mornings and go to my other job in school administration in the afternoon. But actually I find work here is always on my mind. It becomes a part of me.

What reputation does the centre have in the immediate neighbourhood and in Montevideo as a whole?

Oh, that's quite a funny story. The proprietor of the chemist's opposite here is very indignant. He really hates us. If one of us goes in there, he starts hurling insults at us before we've even bought anything. He seems to feel personally attacked by what we represent. Whenever he's got a spare moment he's at the window spying on us. We certainly don't go unnoticed. Lots of passers-by ring us up to say they saw the sign and would like to know what we do and whether we need any help.

Men as well as women?

Yes. Of course we get a few psychopaths, but that's rare. In Montevideo we're pretty well-known. But we've also received letters from people in the interior of the country who've read about us in the daily newspaper, *La República*. So we now have a project for the interior, where the problem is even more serious than here because the women are more marginalised; ignorance is much greater and *machismo* is more marked. Not an ounce of feminism has ever been introduced there. To organise anything there is obviously very difficult for us. We have to drive out at weekends. In this respect I'm lucky because my partner works in the fishery and is often away from home for days on end. So I can plan my own time more independently. Basically, our centre is now very much respected, although at first many people from both sexes were rather uncertain about it, mainly because it was associated with the word, feminism. But we've de-mystified this word; we've explained what we do in real terms and today people do know *SOS Mujer.*

Does SOS Mujer *see itself as part of the feminist movement?*

No, for quite valid reasons we don't describe ourselves as feminists because the feminist movement still gets attacked in Uruguay. It's quite common for movements to start off on a very radical footing with no attempt to water down their message. I'm not criticising that at all, just accepting it as a sociological fact. The other thing about the feminist movements is that they've been imported. A lot of people were in exile and when they returned from Switzerland, Sweden, Germany or from Mexico they wanted to bring their experience of these different countries back with them, to a country whose society is predominantly influenced by *machismo* and by our sexist upbringing and a *macho* control over the nature of relationships between men and women. In this environment feminist ideas are bound to be rejected.

We're concerned here with violence against women. We work with battered wives, with women who've become the victims of their husbands or male members of the family. But we haven't met all our objectives just by being a safe haven after the acts of violence have occurred. Instead, we want to change public awareness of this problem and assist in the process of enlightenment. There shouldn't be any more battered women in this society. Our work is directed at society as a whole. It's no use just changing the women, the other half of society has to be changed as well. So it's important that our work is also directed at men. It's precisely for this reason that we don't define our group as feminist. On the other hand, any member of the group can obviously describe herself as a feminist if she wants to.

Violence is a very serious problem here. That's why we have to proceed very cautiously. We have to be careful we don't expose ourselves to attack through carelessness. So when we speak to the press or give lectures, we always make it clear that we're not against men, we're for society as a whole, for both sexes. We always have to play this up a bit and be flexible in our approach to the sensitive issue of men's violence. We establish one thing right at the start of every radio broadcast and every event: Dear people, it's not a question of feminism or *machismo* but a question of violence. That usually manages to break the ice.

Footnotes

[1] Lady is a first name, not a title.

Eulalia Yagarí González (Colombia)

The right to love and politics: an indigenous activist's perspective

In Colombia indigenous people are in the minority. They number around 600,000 - around two to three per cent of the population - and are divided into some sixty different ethnic groups. Eulalia Yagarí González is a Chami Indian. Geographically speaking, the Chami are one of the Choco Indian groups concentrated on the slopes of the Western Cordillera stretching to the Pacific plain. An estimated 5,000 Indians of the Chami tribe are scattered across Colombia, of which 1,100 live in Cristiania in the Antioquia region, the Indian community Eulalia Yagarí comes from. The Chami have retained their own language which has its roots in the Embera language. 'I speak, sing, dance and compose songs and poems in Chami,' says Eulalia.

Eulalia Yagarí is convinced that the struggle of Colombian Indians for land, culture and autonomy must be conducted on many different fronts simultaneously. At the parliamentary elections in October 1991 she fought for a seat in the senate on the slate of the *Alianza Social Indigena* (Indigenous Social Alliance). However, only the leader of the list was elected, Anatolio Quira, one of the first of three indigenous senators in Colombia to take office. Colombia's new constitution passed in July 1991 has finally awarded the indigenous communities recognition and legal concessions. For the first time Colombian society has been defined as multi-cultural and multi-ethnic and the collective indigenous land rights are to be respected. But there is a stark contrast between reality in Colombia and what is laid down in the constitution and law. The continuing pauperisation of indigenous communities and the physical threat of massacre and murder as a result of land disputes suggest that five centuries of exploitation are not yet over.

Eulalia Yagarí's struggle is not only relevant to Colombian indigenous communities but to all oppressed people, particularly women. As a woman and a politician she suffers from the incompatibility of political demands with those of her personal life. The incessant state of war has almost managed to destroy the latter.

* * * * * * * * * * *

*How would you describe the role of Indian women historically compared
with their position in the indigenous movement today?*

We Indian women in Colombia were key participants in the development
of our societies right from the start, before Columbus invaded America.
Across the American continent we helped lay the foundations of our societies
and create their economic, social, cultural and religious structures. Indian
women also bore witness to the conquerors' attempts to massacre and
exterminate our peoples. We resisted. We fought against them with inferior
weapons, hurled poisoned spears and arrows at them, and poured boiling
water on them to burn their faces. We joined in the killing and we also
raised our voices and denounced the crimes of the Spanish. I'm thinking in
particular of a courageous woman, Kazikin La Gaitana. In 1540 when
Pizarro invaded Popayan and had her son burned alive, Kazikin gathered
the indigenous people around her: from the Paeces, Guambianos and
Coconuco peoples and from other Indian tribes. She succeeded in rallying
the support of important people ruling the Indian provinces at that time.
After some time they managed to capture her son's murderer. She avenged
the crime by tying up Pizarro's envoy, gouging out his eyes and slowly
dismembering him. La Gaitana was taking her revenge for everything that
had been done to the indigenous peoples, in particular the women, the
source of life, the ones who have maintained the education, culture, tradition
and religion of our peoples.

Indian women were always integrated into the work process in our
communities throughout the American continent and throughout Colombia.
So we still take an active part in production even today. We Indian women
never sleep in and we never stay at home. We can be found in agriculture,
in education and in healthcare. Equally, Indian women play an active role
in political meetings, even when their right to this is barely recognised by
our own community leaders. Simply to be acknowledged and heard in their
own communities, Indian women have to be very attentive and persistent.
They have to keep up a constant struggle for their own space. Indian women
and, in fact, all women in America and Europe have to overcome a lot of
opposition if they want to be acknowledged in society and get involved
politically.

Why did you agree to be an Indian candidate for the senate elections?

Before I answer your question, let me just say that the political
participation of Indian women is nothing new. We've always been involved

in politics in the sense that we've always defended our interests, our tradition, our culture, our fellow men as well as our whole people and our land. We fought for 500 years until our voices were finally heard. Now Colombia has a new constitution. A certain sector of the Indian population, the blacks and other ethnic groups have united in a political alliance, which will not only defend Indian interests and rights, but also those of the blacks, the lower classes - in fact all marginalised groups. When they were looking for candidates and they noticed that I'd been politically active for twelve years and was committed to the rights of women, children and our entire people, they chose me. Actually I only agreed to the candidature after they approached me for the third time. But as an Indian woman I don't just want to fight for the interests of Indian women, I also want to fight for the rights of all women in this society, the workers, the *campesinas*, the black women who've always been discriminated against until now, the women of other ethnic groups like the gypsies - basically all women who are politically and socially active in this country. But when I demand their rights I don't just want to make superficial political speeches. No, if I get elected to the Senate, I'll fight for quite specific proposals and projects promoting the social development of women: the right to antenatal care, for recognition of women's participation, and power for women to achieve their right to work and decent jobs, not just jobs that are almost beyond physical endurance.

What could indigenous women achieve in the senate if they were elected?

We could start by implementing everything the new constitution has assured us of. We must form alliances with other progressive forces, with specific groups on the left, but also on the right. We'll see what the politicians will actually do. Of course, in the election campaign, they promised all sorts of things. Personally I don't have any illusions about what I can do for the Colombian people, firstly because I'm aware of my limitations and secondly because we don't have the financial means. We have far too little power in the state to really change society. All I can do is simply devote all my strength and intelligence to the task in hand. I'll also use my feminine cunning, because in all honesty, we women are very cunning. Women are capable of a great deal. It's just that we've always been undermined. Our rights were taken away from us and we were undervalued. Women were there for sex, child-rearing and maybe the odd bit of politics. We never had any more space than that. So we're well-placed to flirt with our bodies, but also with our intelligence, our discerning nature and with our cunning. We have many abilities we can use to change this society. As an Indian woman I can't speak such high class Spanish as a big politician, but that doesn't mean I have no right to be heard. Despite all my limitations, I intend to fight in the senate - albeit cautiously, because the senate is a completely new ball game for us.

You just said you only let yourself be nominated as a candidate after the third invitation. Why were you so hesitant initially and why did you accept in the end?

Basically I never wanted to get into big politics. I've been pushed into it. The work in the senate seemed to me like the struggle of a little fish faced with a shark. And besides, this work means giving both my daughters to someone else to look after. I've also got a partner who's politically active as well. I have a difficult relationship with him. We love each other but our political struggle in this quagmire of violence and war makes it impossible for couples to live in peace with one another. We're not the only ones in this position in Colombia. Hundreds of us women, Indian women, *campesinas*, women from the popular movements, workers and trade unionists aren't able to have happy relationships with their partners. Commitment to the cause takes away the ability and time for love. Relationships often break up, because there's a lack of opportunity for the joys and pleasures of love, affection and togetherness. Sometimes we're only at home for one or two days and often only for one night. There's no time to sleep with each other or even just stroll along the street together. And there's no time to keep the family together or bring up the children properly.

How have you solved the problem with your children?

Oh, that's a sad story. I have to sneak the time, so to speak, to write my daughters a two- or three-page letter. I always tell them: 'Patricia, I love you so much. Are you studying hard? I'm always thinking of you' and 'Marcela, I feel stronger just knowing you are there.' In some ways I think I only do my work for them. Sometimes I feel a creeping desire to give up political work completely and devote myself entirely to my children. That's when I hope they can replace me at some point. I'm thirty-two now. I'm not going to be able to bring about big social change. Some things are still in a bad way as regards the process of unity in Colombia. I think my daughters need a good education. But not even that would make up for what they've had to do without in the last few years. Over the past ten years I've only been with them now and then.

Who are your children growing up with?

With relatives. But of course an aunt or granny can't replace a mother. You can't just switch emotional ties. Traditionally, we Indian woman always have our children with us. Indian children grow up differently from other children. From birth we carry children around with us. In many communities they're only weaned when they're five or six. I suckled Marcela for four years. Because of my work I had to wean Patricia after two years. I think this long and close relationship early on helps Indian communities to develop a strong sense of solidarity. We may well have political differences, but we still feel ourselves to be indigenous people. Today our children, the children of the popular leaders, are growing up with traumas and psychological problems as a result of the permanent state of war. They have no home, no parents who love each other, they don't feel protected and they don't have a good education. Lots of children are constantly in day nurseries. We leaders and women at the head of the popular movements sometimes find ourselves on our own in the end, not because of the political work in itself, but because it's being conducted in a war situation. To make real progress as leaders, things would have to be more humane and this physical and mental state of war would have to end. The way it is at the moment we're always exhausted, we get embittered and we age quickly out of pure sorrow. Often you don't know how to go on because of all the insecurity around you. And then there's the constant worry you might be murdered.

Perhaps that's also one of the reasons why there are so many rock groups in Colombia at the moment. I think young people's fury and resentment is expressed in this music. They rock, they shout. Others take drugs. I'm quite concerned about young people growing up in this state of neglect. That's why part of our political programme in the 'red zones', the areas of political conflict in our country, is to encourage leisure projects and include rock music, for example, in skills training work. I think it's wonderful to see rock groups in Latin America making a stand against the 500 year celebrations. Here in Medellín alone there are two or three groups. In October, at the height of the campaign against these celebrations, they're going to go on stage a few times to promote our cause.

What do you think are the main issues in the campaign against the celebrations?

As you know, the Spaniards came to America to spread fear and terror, to take their country away from the inhabitants and even change the names of the places and people and finally to force their religion, their politics and their culture on them. Obviously we can't blame all Spaniards *per se* for this, it was Queen Isobel, the Catholic kings, the rulers of Spain at that time. Spain was also poor in those days. I know there are still political prisoners in Spain today. If we're against the 500 years celebrations it's not directed against all the Spanish but more specifically against the elite who've always seen themselves as the lords and masters and still do today. I'm against the celebrations because I've gradually come to understand that the same misery of 500 years ago is reproduced over and over again here. The demands I want to present in the senate all have their particular place in this 500 years campaign. In this campaign we're taking the lid off our history of conquest, evangelisation, persecution. We're saying no to ignorance and violence in a country that's ranked as one of the most violent countries in Latin America alongside Nicaragua, Guatemala and Honduras. In fact, our demands are valid in any country in which people are striving for social change and suffer repression as a result.

Do you have any special training for your current political work?

No. I never had the opportunity to go to secondary school or sit school leaving exams or go to university. My political training consists of what I've learnt in the communities. Beyond that I've always been interested in everything. I've talked to all sorts of people and I've found out about things like anthropology, sociology and psychology. I've learnt that being involved in politics means a lot more than defending the interests of a political party. As far as learning is concerned, I'm like an ant rummaging about and digging up knowledge. If I'm now a senatorial candidate, that's got nothing to do with my formal education. It's more to do with my people realising what type of experience I'd had and how I'd worked. At 19 I only had two years of elementary school. When I was 21 I finished year five in five months, just after I'd given birth to my eldest daughter.

Is your mother tongue Chami?

Yes. I grew up bilingual in Spanish and Chami. I also sing, dance, write songs and poems in Chami!

You're a member of the Organisation of Antioquia Indigenous Peoples (OIA). What type of women's programme do you have in the OIA?

We don't have a specific women's programme which reflects the fact that very few women are in leadership positions. Cristiania is an Indian community where many politicians like to have a finger in the pie. Women have achieved a lot of political space but many are not in a position to take on political functions. In my opinion we need a new policy for liberating women, but I don't mean a policy like the ones introduced here from Europe and North America. The cultures and societies are totally different there. For example, there's a presumption here that French women go to bed with anyone - before AIDS existed, of course. I don't mean to denigrate French women, quite the opposite. My positive image of women is not just limited to Indian women. I feel that women in general are amazing, lovely creatures. Women - Indian and black women, French, Cubans, Soviet citizens, Chinese women - all women are the most beautiful people in the world.

On the other hand, some women who used to suffer and were repressed and put up with being beaten, have managed to liberate themselves. But what happened? They now act like they're on another planet and behave just like men. I know it's great to feel free at last. But do we really want this type of freedom? I don't think so. I want liberated women to strive for something different. Women must change the course of this universe. But to do this we're going to need all our willpower. In our countries there's a giant economic, religious and cultural heritage which we can use to our advantage - but we also have to respect it. I mean, here in Cristiania a woman who has never been in public life is far from being the same as an emancipated popular leader. It would be wrong to disregard such differences and take freedoms for ourselves which other women don't understand. If we don't want to irritate other women, but work with them politically, we have to be cautious.

Let me give you an example, when women feel the need for a physical relationship, we shouldn't carry it on in full public view. Even on the Left, men are just waiting to shoot their mouths off about you and claim that's all women are there for. In Latin America *machismo* exists everywhere, even among men who call themselves revolutionaries. But they're only revolutionary on the street; at home they beat their wives or at the very least forbid them to speak. But there's no point in openly attacking this *machismo*. Instead, we have to begin with education, in the day-nurseries and the schools.

How do you defend yourself personally, then, against machismo?

Well, I've had to put up with all kinds of stuff. There are stupid, uncouth types who shout at you and don't let you finish speaking. So you have to grit your teeth and say to them: 'listen, you may be physically stronger, but I've got more inside my head. And if we're seriously fighting for the same cause, then no one just gives orders and no one just obeys.' On the political circuit I've put up with some difficult situations. If they're travelling with a woman as a member of a delegation, the men are right in there trying to go to bed with her. And afterwards they've got nothing better to do than talk about it and then it becomes the latest gossip. 'Oh, so you went to bed with her, as well? And what was she like?' After that the woman is finished politically. A friend of mine was done for because 15 men claimed to have slept with her. And they laughed themselves stupid over it. That's *machismo* in its purest form. As a woman involved in politics, you still have to deal with stuff like that.

You know, it happens to me sometimes too, that I like some guy and I'd just like to sleep with him and have a physical relationship. Can you imagine what kind of fear I have to go through afterwards about what the others are going to say? These prejudices, this moral preaching... The insults a woman would get if she'd slept with thirty men and wanted to go into political life... They don't bear thinking about... You really have to choose your partner very carefully. He has to like you as a woman, he must value your political work and he mustn't just be out for his own orgasm. I've suffered a lot from that in my relationships. If I'm not feeling anything, then I protest volubly. I don't let that happen to me. It's a right which we women all share. When it comes down to it, for women the struggle is not just about economic changes; it's about feeling loved and respected, feeling like women in the most comprehensive sense of the word.

But we can't wage this struggle the same way everywhere. You have to go about it differently when you're dealing with women who think of themselves as the skivvy at home and nothing else. In this country there are still a lot of women who believe they can't experience any sexual pleasure because that's simply a man's prerogative. Many allow themselves to be repressed by their husbands all their lives without even realising it.

Don't you think that's gradually changing?

Certainly there are women who think the same way I do and are working towards a different educational policy. But it's not just a question of discussing things with men because men as individuals and the system which represses are not one and the same thing. Men are also our lovers, our friends and our brothers. The problem is that in Colombia and in the whole of Latin America there are still far too few men who acknowledge our true worth.

What will you do if you don't get into the senate?

I'll work in the communities again. I have a piece of land I'll cultivate. I enjoy tilling the soil, sowing, harvesting. I'm actually a *campesina*. I used to grow coffee. I worked hard at it and carried heavy loads. But with the money I earned, I used to buy myself nice clothes. I'd happily do that again.

Postscript

In the regional elections Eulalia Yagarí was elected as a member of Antioquia's regional parliament on 8 March, 1992 (International Women's Day!).

FEMINIST PUBLICATIONS

Zoila Hernández (Peru)

Mujer y Sociedad: writing for a mass audience

The Peruvian women's periodical, *Mujer y Sociedad* (Women and Society), appears as a monthly supplement in the daily newspaper, *La República*, with a circulation of over 100,000 copies. *Mujer y Sociedad* is by no means the only feminist women's periodical in Latin America which appears in this format. *La Doble Jornada* in Mexico or *Nosotras* and *Lawray* in Bolivia also appear as supplements in progressive daily or weekly newspapers. The advantages of this are obvious: the periodicals solve their sales problems and reach a wide readership over and above active and organised feminists. In these types of magazines current and important issues for feminists have to be presented in such a way as to be interesting to the female readership as a whole. This is all the more difficult as the female publishers of these magazines only have limited knowledge of the impact they are making or the number of female readers they are actually reaching. I spoke to Zoila Hernández, the editor of *Mujer y Sociedad* about this question.

* * * * * * * * * *

How did the periodical Mujer y Sociedad *come about and why did you decide to publish it as a supplement in the daily newspaper,* La República*?*

The magazine was first published in July 1980. The popular movements were very active at that time and the trade unions considered themselves to be the vanguard. The unions put women's demands right at the bottom of the list. We were a small group of women who wanted to inform people about women's rights, to win political space for women and have a social presence. So we put the first edition together and aimed to distribute it throughout Peru. We thought that with this magazine we could prove how much strength and talent women can muster. At the same time we wanted to differentiate ourselves from the existing political and trade union movements which had no national newspapers, but only little booklets which were handed out to their own respective members.

We soon came up against the usual difficulties. We didn't have a penny. Every one of us contributed from our own pockets as far as we were able. I was a lecturer at the university, others were teachers. We hoped to recoup some of the money through the sales of the magazine. It was like that until 1985. We always planned to publish four issues a year but it was never more than two, in 1984 only one. In 1985 we sent off proposals to try to get some financial backing. We had an acceptance from Holland and they agreed to give a little financial support to the magazine and to courses for poor and working class women. The idea of running courses had come up because we were forever being invited to lectures and information events. At that time we always dedicated the magazine to one theme per issue; violence against women, female sexuality, women in history, and people valued our expertise in these themes. So on top of our editorial work four or five of us were also giving lectures. We totally wore ourselves out.

With the financial support, we were able to maintain a greater continuity in the publication of the magazine. But by the end of 1987 we realised that the magazine in its present form had reached its limit of four issues per year. So we invited women working in the alternative media field to a meeting and discussed two options: either continue working together in future on this limited basis or attempt to penetrate the mass media. In the end we decided we wanted to extend our circulation beyond small women's groups and try to enter the mass media world with twelve issues a year. The time was ripe for us, what with all the information we'd collected on the women's movement in the meantime. The editor of *La República* had a look at our magazine and was won over to our ideas. That was a great triumph for us. The commercial, democratic press had accepted us. Since then *Mujer y Sociedad* has appeared as a monthly supplement in a newspaper with a national distribution and circulation of between 100,000 and 120,000 copies. Just imagine, now we get letters from parts of the country we've never even visited. Peasant women from Puno even ordered six subscriptions for six groups in their community!

So is it also possible to order the periodical separately?

Of course. A portion of each issue is used as the supplement. The rest is sent off on request or by subscription, mainly to Europe. We also distribute a lot free to schools and women's organisations that we work with. And then we're often asked to give away free copies at various events.

Is Mujer y Sociedad *now self-financing?*

No, but at least we've made a name for ourselves on the information scene. Our readership consists of women in the media, women at the university and teachers, as well as housewives and women leaders in the poor and working-class sectors. And of course the usual newspaper readership, because we do address men specifically when we're writing about things like personal relationships, which partner should use contraceptives or get themselves sterilised, reproductive rights, general health or violence. Young people are also particularly important to us.

Do you get any kind of feedback? How do you know that you're not just writing into the blue, considering that the bulk of each issue is sold automatically with La República?

We get letters from readers. We've reserved an extra page in the magazine for them. Another indicator is that almost all the women's organisations in the provinces have renewed their subscriptions. Our main problem at the moment is that the magazine is very much oriented towards the urban population. We want to be able to work in the provinces in the future. But the editors really need to travel to the different regions and get to know the specific situation in each place before they can write about it.

It's also clear we're quite important when there are cases of discrimination against women and we're asked by various organisations and groups to publicise it. We acted as the mouthpiece for various women's groups in 1989 when the issue of the decriminalisation of abortion in rape cases came up within the context of the new penal law. Unfortunately, the then president, Alan García, bowed to the Church's opinion on the matter.

How are you going to solve your financial problems?

For some time now we've been trying to sell advertising space because the magazine really has to be self-supporting at some stage. Obviously in this catastrophic economic situation we have in Peru, it's not easy to persuade factories manufacturing women's clothing or businesses selling women's accessories or fitted kitchens to place ads in our magazine. Nevertheless we always manage to get one or two adverts and each one earns us a cool US$500. Of course it takes a lot of effort. We certainly wouldn't bias our contents in favour of an advertiser for the sake of getting an advert. Each one of our issues is seen as a contribution to the creation of a different and democratic society in which peace and justice will prevail and the rights of women are ensured. We regard ourselves as open and pluralistic, which wasn't always the case. At times we've been sectarian. But in view of the present crisis, we now believe we can't change anything by confining ourselves to the women's movement. We have to make an impression on other circles of society.

What do you mean, other circles?

I'll give you an example. Along with women's organisations like *Manuela Ramos*, *Flora Tristán*, or *Aurora Vivar* we are members of a permanent women's forum which meets once a month and where events of national importance are supposed to be coordinated, together with female members of parliament from the left and the right. Women who have completely different political concerns have now become more sensitive to women's issues. There's a woman called Lourdes Nano from the *Partido Popular Cristiano* (PPC), who's a member of parliament for a completely reactionary party, but nevertheless she stood up for women's rights when she was challenged about the issue of violence against women[1]. Mercedes Cabanillas from the former ruling party, APRA, wants to make rape within marriage a criminal offence, which we totally agree with, but which the men in her party don't understand at all. Beatriz Merino from the *Movimiento Libertad* (Freedom Movement), supports women's right to apply for loans so they can solve their financial problems and demands the right to equality of political participation. Certainly these women are playing the role of outsider within their own political parties. They've even admitted in interviews for our magazine that their own parties are heavily influenced by *machismo*.

It's important for us to reach agreement on certain issues if we're to practise politics effectively. And there are few enough women in parliament. The Left has only got three women MPs. The Right actually has more. I think that institutions like the permanent women's forum are well-suited to contributing answers to Peru's crisis from the female perspective. My hope is that MPs will introduce our demands or launch their own attacks in parliament while we actively support them from the outside. But I won't deny that we've discussed the pros and cons of such a forum in great depth. It's quite likely that our sense of common purposes will be shot to pieces over the abortion issue.

How would you assess the value of such an initiative in Peru?

I think we women are the ones who've taken a step which goes far beyond what the political parties have to offer at the moment. Because really they're doing nothing more than defending their own political territory. They only act within their own reference points and in doing so they just mark time. Peru won't emerge from its current crisis if forces aren't united. I think the moment is past when you could still afford to fight about who has truth on their side.

Hasn't women's position in Peru been affected by the crisis in the Left internationally?

No, I don't think so, precisely because the women's movement has fought for its autonomy for ten years. That doesn't mean that the women's movement doesn't also include women who are in left-wing parties as well. But they're wise enough today, as far as I can see, not to mix these two roles. Of course the crisis of the Left can have an effect on women's groups when parties approach them directly and try to enlist their support. That happened with the glass-of-milk programme, for example, in the Coma district, where there were some pretty dirty tricks and the women in the committees were finally divided along party political lines. Absurd! In the end, most of the women didn't even vote for the Left!

Getting back to Mujer y Sociedad, *it's not the only women's periodical in Peru. Doesn't the existence of several periodicals reduce the readership for each of them?*

Mujer y Sociedad isn't the only one, but it's the only one in Peru which appears every month with a mass circulation. In any case there's no competition because all the magazines are very different. *Viva* which is put together by the *Flora Tristán* women's centre appears a lot less frequently, is more comprehensive and analytically orientated, and aimed rather more at small women's groups. They're trying to make people more sensitive to feminism, but we're trying to reach the masses. *La Tortuga* comes out three or four times a year. It's better produced and more expensive and is aimed primarily at women in decision-making posts, a female elite. And that's also quite okay. For me the only problem is that the other magazines don't appear frequently enough and only have a small circulation of about 3 or 4,000. As far as women's issues are concerned, I think we need to cover all sides.

Does La República *reserve the right to make editorial changes of any kind?*

No, not at all. That was an essential condition for us.

Without the guarantee of distribution via the daily newspaper would you have any chance of getting advertising?

No, certainly not.

You just mentioned kitchen or women's fashions as possible adverts. Aren't you simply emphasising women's traditional role in this way?

We used to think we shouldn't accept that kind of advertising. But we see things differently today. Obviously, if you could only see a woman's behind in the advert we'd immediately reject it or suggest the company change the advert. What's crucial is that women's bodies shouldn't be turned into sexual objects. But you know, it's typical of us to mix the traditional, the modern and what we're still seeking, our utopia. In Lima there are many people who think that feminists are 'superwomen'. But that's not true at all. We Peruvian feminists are faced with a lot of contradictions from day to day; we reject being chained to the home and yet every day we're good, submissive housewives. And don't think we get any help from our male partners, if we have them. We're the ones who worry about whether the children get something to eat after school, not them. The husbands of feminists aren't an inch more progressive than other husbands.

At the end of the day the so-called ultra-modern woman carries exactly the same absurdities of Peruvian society around with her as the woman from the glass-of-milk programme or the literacy course. You see, women from the poor neighbourhoods go to their committees full of self-awareness to inform themselves about contraception but then they're still afraid they'll be beaten by their husbands when they get home late. Perhaps those are precisely the elements that bind us women with different social backgrounds together: we all have a hard time opening up, we've all received emotional and physical knocks, and we've all failed to be acknowledged as people. I suspect the feeling of commonality between feminists and women from the popular movements in Latin America is greater than in Europe because of this joint heritage - once you replace the popular movement which doesn't exist in Europe with other non-feminist sectors.

If you compare European periodicals with Mujer y Sociedad *do you see differences or common strands?*

When it comes to the contents, certainly the differences aren't so great, especially the treatment of various cultural and historical issues where the aim is to make women more visible. But as regards publishing technology, we're on completely different planes. And that's a reflection of the worldwide technological divide between North and South. We use basic newspaper paper, print predominantly in black and white, seldom have expensive advertisements. Most women's magazines in Europe have a high-gloss finish, and are fully financed...

I wish that were true!

OK so not all of them. Your style and the lay-out are also completely different. We've got more tropical styles. There's more movement on the page with us. A photo can also be angled sometimes, a headline at the top, in the middle or at the bottom. Your style is always straight, straight, straight. A magazine is also a work of art.

Footnotes

[1] In March, 1991 Lourdes Nano introduced a bill in Parliament about violence against women.

Lucy Garrido and Lilian Abracinskas (Uruguay)

Cotidiano Mujer: a platform for the women's movement

Founded in 1985, *Cotidiano Mujer*, is aimed at women from Montevideo's political left who are either politically active feminists or are interested in feminism. In September 1991 Lucy Garrido and Lilian Abracinskas from *Cotidiano Mujer* came to Germany to find out more about the work of feminist magazines in Europe. Their visit prompted an interesting debate about the differences and similarities between feminist media in the two continents.

* * * * * * * * *

Presumably your magazine belongs to Uruguay's alternative media?

Lilian: You know, I've often heard this word 'alternative' in Europe. I suspect that often what's actually meant by that is something like 'badly organised'. By 'alternative' we mean a work and communication project or a model of resistance which we carry out as well as we can, whereas the description 'alternative' is often used as an excuse with you. *Cotidiano Mujer* is alternative for us because the magazine doesn't belong to the mass media and is feminist.

How long has this periodical existed?

Lilian: The first issue of *Cotidiano Mujer* appeared in September 1985, straight after the end of the dictatorship. There were six or seven of us women then, who ventured out into the open for the first time, like other women's groups in Uruguay at that time. We wanted to create a forum and a medium of communication for the women's groups. Women had already been active in the resistance during the dictatorship, but it was only in 1985 that women's groups suddenly started springing up.

Were you a journalist?

Lilian: No. Lucy, our only professional journalist, hadn't yet joined us.

Lucy, why did you quit your job with other newspapers?

Lucy: For political reasons. During the dictatorship I worked on a weekly magazine which I respected at the time. Some of my female colleagues came from the Left and some were followers of the *Colorado* party (traditional bourgeois party). Obviously the *Colorados* were against the military, just like the lefties. Then the elections came along and everyone started to show their true colours. The *Colorados* used the magazine for their own electioneering. That's why a lot of lefties quit. I joined a Communist daily newspaper. But then I had a row with them too...

Lilian: And then you came to us. We set out from the start as a group of women activists and amateur journalists. Some people had worked in health, others had been active in trade unions or party politics. Quite simply we wanted to speak from a women's perspective about all the women's issues which had been hushed up for so long. The first issue was published with the financial support of an Italian woman living in Uruguay. After that the magazine lasted for three years without any outside financing. Of course, we had to earn our living elsewhere. The last issue of this period appeared in November, 1989. We'd always sold the magazine as cheaply as possible so every woman could afford it. This meant we had a monthly deficit of thirty per cent and we ended up without a single peso. So we didn't publish the magazine again until November 1990, though we did broadcast a radio programme instead from March to December, for one hour every day.

Did you have to buy the air time?

Lucy: No, but we weren't paid either. It was 'Radio 30', the communist radio station. One of the chief editors there is a good friend of ours. She was prepared to take the risk and see what happened. Of course, there'd never been anything like it before. It all went as well as it could have. But in December, 1990, it came to an end because the station was in financial straits - even though it was one of the most popular stations in the whole country.

Would you have gone on broadcasting otherwise?

Lucy: Oh, we have anyway. This year we broadcast a programme once a week on another station. But actually our plans are heading in another direction. At the moment we're looking for financial backing to set up a daily four-hour radio show with the editor we worked with in the beginning.

Isn't the magazine enough for you?

Lilian: No. You see, the basic problem is this: in the early days the magazine was affordable and immediately accessible to all women. Now we're publishing a more theoretical magazine. Obviously, there's also light-hearted stuff, interviews and a humorous column. But its aim is to offer the Uruguayan women's movement a theoretical platform.

So wouldn't this platform exist without your magazine?

Lilian: Of course not. There's no other magazine of this type. We get very little reading material from abroad and when we do, most women can't afford it.

Do you disseminate foreign feminist theory? What about Uruguayan feminism?

In unison: We do both. Obviously it's not just us on our own as a handful of women editors. We get contributions from outside, from feminist academics, for example.

What else is there in the feminist magazine world in Uruguay?

Lucy: Very little. Apart from us there's a weekly women's supplement in the daily newspaper, *La República*, called *La República de las Mujeres*. Incidentally, the idea for that originally came from us. A few women from *Cotidiano Mujer* collaborated on this supplement for about a year because we thought we could achieve a mass circulation for feminist journalism that way. After disagreements with the owner of the newspaper, though, we withdrew.

So your experience was a negative one in the end?

Lucy: No, I wouldn't say that. Our withdrawal was prompted by a boycott of the newspaper by the workers - we ended our collaboration out of solidarity. Nowadays the wife of the newspaper owner is the editor of the supplement and so the contents have become pretty commercial.

Lilian: One thing you have to bear in mind is that *La República de las Mujeres* is a twelve-page supplement, not a magazine. The circulation is 40,000, whereas ours is 1,500. Our main complaint is that the supplement is a commercial venture.

Could you imagine a feminist supplement where that was different? Don't you always have to cater for 'popular taste', if you're working within a commercial medium?

Lucy: No, not necessarily. For a year, *La República de las Mujeres* worked. We still managed to write something that was thoroughly appealing.

So market forces aren't so restrictive after all?

Lucy: I just think it's possible to combine the commercial side with a good product.

But you're not going to get involved again at the moment?

Lucy: If a new paper were launched, then yes.

Lilian: We don't think cooperation with *La República* makes sense any more. It's entirely given over to sensationalism; controversial issues simply don't get a mention.

Lucy: Lesbians, for example. Or abortion: when they mention abortion, they publish one article in favour of it and one article against it. They're not prepared to take sides.

Lilian: They hide behind an alleged credo of journalistic objectivity. Not that it means a great deal, incidentally. Ever since we've stopped working there, our opinions don't get a mention. A book Lucy published with another woman hasn't ever been mentioned in the supplement, even though there's a column on new publications. The relaunch of *Cotidiano Mujer* in November 1990 didn't get a mention either.

You said the idea of a women's supplement in La República *that was explicitly a 'women's supplement and not 'feminist' was originally yours. Was it a mark of the women's movmeent's strength or due to the successful efforts of a few women? How did you manage to persuade* La República *to bring out the supplement in the first place?*

Lucy: Both explanations are valid. The owner of the newspaper is really cunning. He calculated that he could take advantage of the trend with a women's supplement from the publicity angle and slap on a price increase.

Lilian: In fact his calculations were proved right for some time. When the supplement appeared on Saturdays the newspaper sold out.

And now?

Lilian: Well, the supplement has got worse and appears on Sundays, the day with the lowest circulation.

Was the idea for a women's supplement taken up by other newspapers?

Lucy: Yes and no. At least in the form of pages for women's issues, though obviously with very traditional contents. You've got to bear in mind the impact of the current economic crisis. Some daily newspapers had to fold, so there's no room for expansion.

Do you publish your magazine to change society or some aspects of it? Or are you serving the needs of a specific sector of women who are already feminists?

Lucy: Well, if we didn't believe in changing society we wouldn't be writing in the first place.

If you compare yourselves with the women and women's magazines you've seen in Europe, do you see similarities or differences?

Lucy: I got to know the editorial collective of a women's magazine in Hamburg and liked them a lot but I felt they were very much writing for a select circle of feminist women. You don't seem to want to broaden your horizons, whereas we want to convince more and more people.

Lilian: You know, *Cotidiano Mujer* is read by both women and men, though admittedly more by those with a left-wing, intellectual stance. The magazine is supposed to be popular; it shouldn't require any great effort to work your way through an article.

How do you organise your distribution?

Lucy: In Montevideo mainly through bookshops and newspaper kiosks and then we have someone who deals with the deliveries. About seventy per cent are distributed like this. In the interior of the country we have contact with women's groups or individual women who distribute copies, though we do intend to distribute to kiosks there as well. We also have some contact with groups in Buenos Aires. We know of other women's magazines in other parts of the continent, but there's no regular cooperation. And that hasn't really changed since the Latin American feminist meeting in November, 1990.

So you don't publish any articles from Argentina, for example, or Peru?

Lilian: Not yet, because we appear bi-monthly and other magazines are often published sporadically, for financial or technical reasons. There's an exchange with women in the media sector: we send them our monthly bulletin and they send us information - it's a sort of network which we call *La Telarana* (spider's web).

Do men work on your magazine?

Lilian: Oh, yes, though not always on the permanent staff - and they have to be good. Recently we ran a series of articles on our *machista* culture to which male journalists and writers contributed.

What are you working on at the moment?

Lilian: Positive discrimination for women in the political system. At a meeting in July the women from the *Frente Amplio*, the Alliance of Parties of the Left, (Broad Front), decided to propose a motion for positive discrimination at the *Frente Amplio's* second congress in August. Afterwards a sort of referendum among the members of the Alliance is supposed to take place following a broad discussion over the coming year. We didn't get the two thirds majority needed to discuss the motion, but the issue isn't over for us, even if we have to settle for a slightly closer approximation between the political participation of women - who are fifty per cent or more of the electorate - and their political representation. We're also looking at how the women's movement can become a real political force, especially in this period of demobilisation in Uruguay.

Lucy: The current left-wing municipal government in Montevideo created a women's coordinating committee, with delegates from the town council, the political parties and six women's groups. They were elected at a women's plenary session. *Cotidiano Mujer* is also represented on the committee. It organises women's workshops on the subject of abortion, violence against women and so on in various neighbourhoods.

What have been the really hot issues for Cotidiano Mujer?

Lilian: An article about Ingrid Strobl[1] or maybe our last issue which interviewed politicians like the head of the communist party, or Fernandez Huidobro of the *Tupamaros*, topics on politics, homosexuality, and then lesbians in March of this year. In the six years of the new women's movement here that subject has never once been openly discussed. Why? Because we're real prudes, incredibly moral types, and because feminists were afraid they'd be called lesbians if they so much as uttered the word. The subject is discussed just as little in the women's groups. Only now are the first lesbian groups being formed in Uruguay. It suddenly occurred to us that we'd published 33 issues of *Cotidiano Mujer* without writing a single word on the subject. So we decided to put the record straight right on the title-page and dedicate a third of the magazine to this important topic. The effect was like dynamite; we even got interviewed on the radio.

Do you get letters from readers?

Lucy: No, almost never. Women phone us or come to the editor's office.

How many women do you have working with you?

Lucy: Five. More women could work here on a voluntary basis, but that doesn't happen much. The Frauenanstiftung[2] finances the newspaper at the moment, to the tune of four hours paid work a day. We don't want our financial backing to turn us into professional feminists.

What does this foreign support mean for you?

Lucy: Obviously we're forever trying to get foreign backing from all over. But we would never accept any editorial interference by our funders. You know, the people in Europe who hand out money basically aren't giving us anything. They're simply giving us back a portion of what they stole from us and appeasing their guilt complexes.

Lilian: Our group wasn't formed because there was financial backing and it won't fall apart if there isn't any anymore. To earn enough to live on, we have to have a second job as well, which means working at least a nine-hour day.

Footnotes

[1] Ingrid Strobl is a German feminist and journalist who has run an international campaign against genetic engineering and new reproductive technology in recent years. From 1987 to 1990 she was imprisoned for her alleged complicity in a terrorist bomb attack in Frankfurt. She was released from prison following successful efforts to prove her innocence.

[2] A German Foundation linked to the Green Party which funds projects employing only women.

Marta Lamas (Mexico)

Debate Feminista: a bridge between academia and activism

Debate Feminista (Feminist Debate), a magazine published in Mexico, differs from the other magazines discussed in this book in that it sees itself explicitly as a theoretical publication. Its design (book format, no photographs or illustrations) makes it clear that *Debate Feminista* is not aimed at a broad readership, but at women (and men) who are interested in the development of feminist theory and discussion. What is striking about *Debate Feminista* is the large number of articles contributed by foreign authors, promoting a vigorous participation in the international feminist debates. Equally interesting is that approximately twenty per cent of the articles published in the magazine are written by (hetero- and homosexual) men. The following is an editorial from the first issue of *Debate Feminista* in March 1990, by Marta Lamas, a veteran of the Mexican women's movement.

* * * * * * * * * *

Debate Feminista tries to respond to feminists' common need for a medium of reflection and debate. It acts as a bridge between academic and political work, a medium to help bring stimulus to research and feminist theory, both within and outside academic institutions, and overcome the rigidity, isolation and detachment of scholarship from the political debate. We don't share the views of the *mujerologas* (specialists in women's issues who are not part of the feminist movement), neither do we agree with 'anti-intellectualism', which has influenced some points of view within the movement. *Debate Feminista* is diametrically opposed to the production of banal studies (and their curricular use) and outbreaks of sentiment in the name of the revolution. Our intention is to analyse the process of political change and work on the creation of a feminist political programme. Living conditions and political structures in Mexico can only be changed through reflection and through theories developed from this reflection.

There are various feminist perspectives in Mexico and contributors on this magazine cannot hope to represent all of them. Nor do we claim to address the entire spectrum of issues within the feminist panorama. Without denying or hiding our differences, what unites us is the desire for a strong, autonomous feminist movement and the urgent need to participate in political debates. Rejecting the concept of a 'feminine being', we believe that the issue of feminism is not women *per se* but the relationship between the sexes. *Debate Feminista* was not created in a void. It is the result of developments within feminism.

There are certainly publications which complement ours, particularly the magazine *Fem* and *Doble Jornada* ('Double Day' - feminist supplement to the daily newspaper, *La Jornada*. To take part in the dialogue with the feminist movement and the other groups in the democratic movement, we want to gather and distribute theory and analyses which do not appear in other publications because of their content, composition or language. Many of the texts we publish are academic but we are also interested in other work: sketches or testimonials, for example. We want to give precedence to texts which are both appropriate and useful for discussion, even if we don't necessarily agree with them. For this reason we also print texts that are hardly known in Mexico at all. Obviously *Debate Feminista* addresses the political process in Mexico, but we also want to consider the international perspective, especially Latin America. We want to build up a network of correspondents across the continent and a translation department as well. *Debate Feminista* is not only a group of editors, activists in the movement take part too. We hope that this union of theory and practice is reflected in the magazine and that it helps us both to communicate political reality and make the dialogue within the movement more fruitful.

The first issue is dedicated to one of the most vital discussions: democracy. Although there have been discussions about a democratic praxis since the early days of the feminist movement, we have not achieved a systematic and rigorous appraisal of its implications or its aims. At best, the different feminist tendencies in Mexico are enmeshed in social and economic issues and at worst are stuck in a *mujer-ist* debate. By *mujerismo* (derived from the word *mujer* - woman) we mean the perception that women possess certain characteristics which make them better than men, simply because they belong to the female sex. Positive discrimination is not part of *mujerismo* since only women are capable of real action and women should therefore only work with women, 'the true supporters of revolutionary change'. We fundamentally disagree with this view. It is only because women as a social group - because of the gender to which they belong - find themselves in specific conditions of discrimination, repression and exploitation, that it is valid to do specific work on their behalf. *Mujerismo* is a disastrous perspective of feminism.

By contrast, a political analysis of the world of women leads us to the following realisation; there is no 'women's cause' which - in itself - unites all women, and not even gender specific issues interest all women at every point in time. The unity of women is not 'natural', but has to be politically created, day after day and through the development of alliances. It is a great challenge to establish a politics for the female sex, i.e. feminist politics, without becoming *mujer-ist*. A feminist, democratic praxis has a difficult balancing act to perform; to work in a specific area (i.e. for the female sex) and at the same time participate in the democratisation of national politics. In our country, however, this has led to some welcome changes: namely, steering away from the concentration on 'the small group' and getting involved in the political reorganisation of the movement. By cutting itself off from political dynamics and concentrating on informal organisation in small groups and personal inititatives, the movement has become incapable of developing an effective long term strategy. We have paid a high political price for divisions and structurelessness within this movement for twenty years in Mexico. And we have paid dearly for the rejection of every institutionalised form of organisation and representation.

Fortunately, the creation of the Mexico City Feminist Coordinating Committee seems to be correcting this tendency. As our everyday life becomes more and more affected by political decisions, the necessity for more effective political action has increased. Although the rejection of political parties has motivated the majority of feminists to look for new forms of action, we have to redefine our politics towards political parties and institutional areas of politics today. The key question is how do we create access to the political arena for ourselves but remain at the periphery of institutional mechanisms? Feminism in our country is divided and disorganised; it has no political presence. So how can we set up an alternative in the political arena which is in harmony with feminist principles and yet is also possible within the rules of the political game? We see the debate about democracy as being crucial to this question.

In *Debate Feminista* we are convinced of the necessity for a fundamental reassessment of what participatory democracy means and what it should include. In 1988 large urban movements were mobilised for democracy while in the nineties, it is more an issue for discussion than a cause for action. How do we participate and where? With many of the urban sectors the issue of participation will probably surface again with the 1991 election campaign. The question is, what options will the feminist movement offer? It is not the only one having difficulty in offering alternatives but its proposals are the least structured. Bearing this in mind, *Debate Feminista* has gathered together various positions from the whole spectrum of the democratic debate. It provides a starting point for discussion and - we hope - for agreement. Unification is a priority.

Berta Hiriart   (Mexico)

mujer/fempress: Latin American women's news agency

The Latin American feminist information service *mujer/fempress* is the most comprehensive of the journalistic projects represented here: an agency and a feminist network at the same time. It would be difficult to compare it with anything similar in Europe. Berta Hiriart, the Mexican correspondent of *mujer/fempress*, belongs to the first wave of Mexican feminism. She was co-founder of the magazines, *La Revuelta* and *fem*, and now also edits the latter. She is a pioneer of women's radio broadcasts, a playwright and an actress. She also acts as an advisor to the teachers' union magazine, *Quehacer de Maestra* (Teachers' Affairs) and is active in the *Alaide Foppa* alternative media centre which mainly produces radio programmes. In the following interview she talks about the outlook and development of *mujer/ fempress*.

* * * * * * * * * *

When was mujer/fempress*' founded?*

The whole thing started in 1981 when a few exiled Chileans, as co-workers at *Instituto Latinoamericano de Estudios Transnacionales*, the Latin American Institute for the Study of Transnationals, (ILET) completed a study of different international women's magazines which they published in a book called *Compropolitan* (a play on the name of the widely-read magazine, *Cosmopolitan*; *comprar* means to buy). Their work on the book opened their eyes to the miserable state of women's image in the mass media. So they founded the *Unidad de Comunicación de la Mujer*, (the Women's Communication Union), as it was called at that time, to create a sort of reverse image of women in the Latin American press, by collecting any articles concerned with the position of women across the continent. In this way the foundations were laid for an interlinking of alternative media dealing with women's issues, but we were still very thin on the ground at that time. A network of correspondents very soon developed which included women from every country in Latin America. The women didn't necessarily have to show any previous journalistic experience, they just had to be in close contact with their respective national women's movements.

I joined the project in 1983 after Viviana Erazo and Adriana Santa Cruz, the co-founders, returned to Chile following the amnesty at that time. They continued their work from there with the support of the *Vicaria de la Solidaridad*, the Vicariate of Solidarity, an ecclesiastical soldarity centre for political prisoners. As you can imagine, that wasn't easy in Pinochet's Chile, or rather Chile under Pinochet. Anyway, we were able to extend our network of co-workers to include Central America where we've only started getting regular reports fairly recently. The Caribbean area is still the missing link.

What are the main aims of mujer/fempress?

We're trying to satisfy two basic needs. Firstly, to facilitate an exchange of ideas between diverse women's groups about what's happening in different countries. They don't have to be women-only groups; they can also be mixed groups. The main thing is they have to prove an anti-sexist standpoint. The problems faced by women from different social sectors are quite similar in the different countries of the continent so it can be very helpful to promote a regular exchange of experiences of victory and defeat on an international level. Another important aspect of our work is to offer alternative material to the media, both the alternative media itself which can't afford agency reports from abroad, and also the mainstream press. That's one of our main concerns: to present women in the mainstream media as active subjects, in charge of their own affairs, and not always simply as caricatures of themselves, as little women. You know what I mean.

So does that mean you don't see yourselves as an alternative agency?

Fempress doesn't sell in that sense. We do work on the basis of subscriptions, but most journalists who republish articles of ours get them free. Naturally, we can only do that with outside financial help, but we now intend to increase the number of subscriptions and somehow adapt to market forces. Of course, you have to see that as part of the whole process: we used to be very humble, knocking on the door of every conceivable editor's office just to get any issue relevant to women accepted in any newspaper, but today there's a different attitude. Sensitivity towards women's issues has increased over the last ten years. So we don't have to ask for any favours, we can now operate from a position of strength and more independently.

What is the regional distribution of your information like? Are there big variations between one country and the next?

Yes, for the simple reason that in many countries alternative media has never existed and so *fempress* has a monopoly, so to speak. It's different here in Mexico. There's heaps of alternative media. Take the daily newspaper, *La Jornada*. They don't have a shortage of information, in fact quite the opposite, they don't know how to process the piles of material they get.

What's your relationship like with the feminist weekly Doble Jornada?[1]

We both publish each other's stuff. You see, our magazine has different sections. One section consists of original contributions from different correspondents about events in various countries, another section has short reports, which are primarily taken up by radio stations - the radio is an important client for *fempress*, and we also retain the cuttings services section which provides articles from from various countries' alternative media. So, to some extent, there's quite an active reciprocal exchange of published material here in Mexico, not only with *Doble Jornada*, but also with the magazine *fem* or with the newspapers of the telephone workers' and teachers' trade unions, newspapers from the provinces, for example *Venceremos* from Morelia, or newspapers from other parts of the country. But despite all this we mustn't forget that our publications still have a sort of ghetto existence. We haven't yet succeeded in really anchoring ourselves in the mainstream media. Really, something like *Doble Jornada* should be superfluous. The reports in this supplement should be accepted by the mainstream daily press, but we simply haven't got that far yet.

Is that because most correspondents in the mainstream press are not yet sensitive to women's issues?

Not only that. It's also because of the decision-making processes of the individual editorial staff. A committed feminist journalist may well have written an interesting article about some women's issue or other, but at the end of the day it's always up to the individual editor to decide what happens to it. Frequently it's then just reduced to a meagre four lines. That's what happened with the famous abortion debate in Chiapas at the end of 1990 which was never reported in the mass media despite intensive work by individual journalists.

Do you have regular meetings as fempress *correspondents?*

Very rarely because it costs a lot of money. On average we meet every three years. The last meeting was in May 1991. Looking back on our work we agreed that for all the similarities between us, big differences do exist from country to country. For example, *fempress* is quoted almost daily by the media in the Dominican Republic, astonishingly enough; there's a particularly widespread use of *fempress* reports in Peru, where there's a long tradition of popular radio stations. In other countries our material largely ends up in the hands of women's groups who use it primarily as educational material or include it in their workshops. The way *fempress* is used varies from place to place, but it's there, that's the main thing.

Footnotes

[1] A feminist weekly supplement to the newspaper, literally translated as 'double working day'.

WHERE NEXT?

Gladys Acosta (Peru)

Feminism and the New World Order

The collapse of socialism in Eastern Europe and the former Soviet Union challenged the left throughout the world, including left-wing feminists who had led their struggle against patriarchal oppression from the perspective of socialist liberation. However degenerate it was, however cynical it sometimes appeared to be and however little it contributed to the liberation of women, socialism in Eastern Europe was, in terms of world politics, the only alternative to capitalism which now goes unchallenged. This is despite capitalism's incapacity to satisfy the basic material needs of a large proportion of the Third World's population. Left-wing and feminist movements that want to bring about real change now have to develop new economic and social programmes which recognise the basic distinction between all people; gender, in other words. This is the demand of Gladys Acosta, a Peruvian feminist who works at *Flora Tristán*, a women's centre in Lima.

* * * * * * * * * *

No one can abstain from the debate about the great historical systems of our time. Not even those of us who are trying to change the complex web of human relationships from a feminist perspective. Everywhere people are talking about the end of ideologies. But before we can grasp the significance of current events and their consequences, we need to pinpoint our various doubts and blank spots. Capitalism is the main pivot of our lives because we were born under its influence. It has a hegemony. Meanwhile for many of us politically aware women, socialism is the starting point of our struggles. But what do we mean by 'socialism'? During 'Perestroika' in the Soviet Union we got very excited about changes in the Eastern Bloc. Now the veils have fallen and we're faced with the naked truth. With some it inspires fear, with others the desire to start again and totally change everything.

Gender, the main distinction between all people, is ignored in most philosophical, political or economic discussions. The reason for this lies partly in the low level of women's participation, but not entirely, because women are not always aware of the system of submission and repression to which we are subjected against our will. We need to find something which unites women in a gender-specific manner. That doesn't mean sweeping under the carpet all the differences between us, like social position, culture or age.

With reference to Nicaragua, Maxine Molineux wrote a very informative article about this issue a few years ago.[1] I share her plea that we take into account women's heterogeneity when discussing women in the revolutionary process, instead of assuming they are homogeneous. Being women doesn't make us 'the same' by any means and yet we do form a social basis. Within this social base there are complex interactions which sometimes lead to conflict. First we need to identify 'strategic women's interests' by which I mean those that question the sexual division of labour and demand a redistribution of housework and childcare, political equality, an end to discrimination, violence and the control of men over women. Strategic women's interests also include the central issue of reproductive rights. While we're in the business of defining terms, I should also mention that there are numerous 'immediate women's interests', which arise from life circumstances and don't necessarily coincide with 'strategic women's interests'. The demands for better living conditions are more influenced by questions of class or ethnicity than by gender. But feminist praxis has to relate to those planes too if we are to secure benefits for all women.

Some countries, including so-called socialist ones, have taken measures to satisfy some of women's immediate interests in order to win their support, without actually changing the balance of power between the sexes in the slightest. The fulfilment of certain demands related to class does not eradicate repression or discrimination. Therein lies the difficulty when the socialist experiment is discussed.

'Failed' but possible socialism

Women's living conditions are a type of social barometer. If we look back at the USSR, Eastern Europe, Cuba or Nicaragua under the Sandinistas, we can see that nowhere has there been effective policies in women's favour. There were attempts to create laws to achieve 'formal equality' but the lives of millions of women were not changed. While they did gain access to paid work, they were never able to share the burden of housework or childcare nor did they gain the freedom to make their own decisions about motherhood, a common characteristic of all these countries. Access to contraception and abortion was permitted for the sake of limiting the birth rate but without explicitly acknowledging it as a human right. The result was limited political participation by women and a failure to penetrate a system which had little understanding of women's demands. It is true that these 'failed' socialist experiments did not count on widespread support from women and criticisms by feminist women's groups were swept under the carpet. These groups had identified the link between women's position and the failure of democratic mechanisms ever since the start of the Russian revolution.

One of the obstacles to a greater feminist development within socialist ideology was Engels' economic theory on women's oppression which prevented Marxist theory from addressing patriarchal relationships in the context of social classes. Women were simply considered part of the proletariat or the bourgeoisie. In other words, this inability to analyse the position of women produced a politics of 'equalisation'; the essentials remained unchanged. The incorporation of women into production without calling the family into question, burdened them all with additional work, as they continued to look after the children, take care of the household and, beyond that, endeavoured to satisfy the demands of production. The image of the 'ideal' family was carried on into the next generation and women continued to be confined to this space. Without wishing to under-estimate the efforts of that generation which fought for freedom, I just want to prevent some errors being made the next time round unless we are giving up hope for a more humane society.

Neo-liberalism in action

For those of us who live under the influence of the capitalist system, the situation is different. When I talk of neo-liberalism, I mean austerity measures, foreign debts, and increased liberties for all those who have the power of money at their disposal and the power of repression over those who make demands. We have now reached a new form of capitalist accumulation. The world's economic system is in a state of change and capital has become more concentrated and centralised. I would not go as far as to say countries don't exist anymore but national identities do certainly play a different role now. It is important to understand the dynamics because otherwise historical responsibilities are obscured and we no longer know whom we're fighting against. If we look at the bare face of neo-liberalism from a women's point of view, we cannot fail to notice its murderous consequences. To create a more humane society we must continue to reject neo-liberalism here and now in the hope of being able to change the dead present into a living future. Under neo-liberalism there is a breathtaking circulation of commodities, but also an exchange of ideas, illusions and dreams. At the moment we're experiencing capitalism's greatest ideological offensive. It's all business: everything is bought and sold and everything has its price. Deals are made even over issues like the massacre in Tiananmen Square; in the UN security council, China abstained at the critical moment in the vote for the use of force in the Iraq Kuwait conflict.

The consequences of neo-liberal politics

We women play an important role in this ever-more internationalised economy because we represent, as ever, a particularly exploitable workforce. A number of studies have revealed the existence of subcontractor chains who work for transnational companies 'informally' and mainly employ women. Basically we are dealing with a kind of integration into the world market which often uses our own homes as its outlet. Obviously, this work is badly paid and completely unprotected and has to be done without any of those social rights which were formerly achieved by trade union struggles. The most important thing for us is to keep hold of just one thread of the enterprise so we can show how the commodities make their way to their final destination. As it advances worldwide, this capitalism also encourages the expansion of certain kinds of tourism. A visible increase in prostitution is part of this, whereby women from poor countries are smuggled into large, internationally-operated rings which exploit them. The reports of Filipina women traded on the West German market send shivers down our spines... What kind of freedom are you talking about there?

How the adoption of austerity measures affects women's lives

It is obvious that foreign debt is one of the most inhuman forms of exploitation in our countries when one considers the ratio between work necessary for workers' needs and work producing profit for employers. The experts have already explained how the prevailing exchange and investment structures have created international finance systems which keep whole populations in inhuman conditions. Although many people might think it crazy, the development model of the global economy has a marked relation to gender. As long as prices were slapped on some luxury consumer items there weren't any serious problems; but now the snares have been set around basic commodities. Women in every household are suffering every day as a result of impoverished economies and those who are most exposed to the effects of foreign debt are women.

When it comes to shopping, caring for sick children or the impossibility of meeting their schooling costs, the illusion of 'leaving poverty behind' evaporates. Yet the problem is not only of an economic nature because under such circumstances the constant tension leads to grave, often lasting exhaustion. The psycho-social damage is alarming. The situation is ready to explode, so to speak... The adoption of austerity measures means a curtailment of the state's commitment to social services with a direct effect on women. Daily life becomes hell for them. The lack of even minimal state welfare presents women (and obviously children too) with crushing working days. There is a constant expenditure of human energy without any hope of rest! No relaxation, no breaks... And if we consider what happens within the family, we notice that women keep the smallest portion of the meagre family income. They give everything to their children or those adults who bring home a pay packet. As a result malnutrition among women is increasing at an alarming rate and their frequent pregnancies represent a superhuman physical achievement.

Women's valiant achievements in defending life and survival are not acknowledged by society. The efforts of women's organisations, whether it be communal kitchens, the glass-of-milk committees or health services don't get the appropriate social esteem. The social value of women cannot be calculated. Perhaps in years to come the fate of millions of women who sacrifice everything to support the children and youth of Peru and other countries in Latin America will be acknowledged. We should not ignore the fact that violence of every form of violence goes hand-in-hand with the difficult situation I have described.[2] It's nothing new for women because the open wounds of sexual violence, abuse at home and the contempt of this *machista* culture, have always featured in our lives and our mothers' lives. The challenge is to prevent these from also affecting our future generations.

And the future?

The neo-liberal offensive is international and demands international opposition strategies combined with political proposals by new social forces which address women's problems. We want to change estimations of our worth and achieve society's acknowledgement of what has been belittled until now as 'women's affairs'. Such important decisions as the right to the termination of unwanted pregnancies can no longer be ignored on the political stage. We want our place in the political decision-making process; we want to have a say in all problems which concern the Peruvian people and the whole world. We want to be informed so as not to be deceived by those who are used to practising politics for a flock of sheep. This road will be difficult but at least we shall regain the strengths of socialism and create social alternatives which are aimed at changing the destructive technological order as well as eliminating the international division of labour and the sexual hierarchy inherent within it. In so doing we shall try to create democratic structures which include the people in the decision-making process. The barriers thrown up by formal representative structures must be overcome urgently. A new democracy should be founded as the basic prerequisite for the society of the future.

Footnotes

[1] Maxine D. Molyneux, 'Mobilisation or Emancipation? Women's interests, state and revolution in Nicaragua', in *Feminist Studies*, vol2, no.2, summer 1985. Updated in R.Fagan et al (ed), *Transition and Development: Problems of Third World Socialism,* Monthly Review Press 1986.

[2] In the last report of the *Comisaria de mujeres in Lima* (the only one in the country at present) 4,800 rapes were filed for 1990, of which 4,200 went to trial. The police commissioner, in reading the document, personally acknowledged the alarming social problem which is posed by the violence of men who are connected to their victims in some way and, which, indeed, persists throughout all levels of society.

Sofia Montenegro (Nicaragua)

The future from a female point of view

The editors of the Nicaraguan monthly magazine *Pensamiento Propio* wanted to hear from the feminist and Sandinista, Sofia Montenegro, what feminism is and what changes it advocates. As publisher and editor-in-chief of the magazine, *Gente* (People), a weekly supplement to the Sandinista daily newspaper, *Barricada*, aimed at young people, Sofia is known in Nicaragua and beyond as someone who speaks her mind, even if in doing so she may undermine the myth of Sandinista heroism. Her answers to the questions from *Pensamiento Propio* are thus refreshingly provocative and read like a programme of feminist principles.

* * * * * * * * * *

What is feminism?

Being a feminist means being a conscious individual with autonomy, self-determination and independence. Women have been robbed of their identity and exploited like other workers.

Is it necessary to have a movement to be a feminist?

Yes, definitely. A woman who denies feminism is either talking nonsense or is simply revealing her alienation. Even women with husbands who degrade them from morning to night can be blind to the seemingly invisible forces which subjugate us women.

So are there a lot of alienated women?

It's true that we feminists are few and far between but we hope that with political and social training, the number of women who know how to promote their own interests and describe themselves as feminists will increase.

Why does feminism have such a bad image?

Because it pushes back frontiers and makes society aware of the image of the obedient woman, subjugated and dominated by the male being. This internalised model of domination prevents a woman from recognising the walls which surround her. Patriarchal society, in which power is masculine, rejects subversive behaviour. A woman who pushes back frontiers and rejects the norm created by man is labelled as someone who breaks the law and is pushed in turn to the periphery of society. She then fights this culture which she accuses of denying her authority.

To what extent is feminism revolutionary?

Feminism is more revolutionary than the entire Left put together and those women who belong to the Left as well as being feminists are even more so. The essence of the feminist ideal is to overthrow all relationships of domination and change all prevailing social and cultural relationships. In Nicaragua we have developed a revolutionary feminism and not a reformist one: revolution at all levels including the home, because you come up against the double standards that many men still have. Heroes and revolutionaries in the line of fire can be total despots at home and no one thinks it wrong. As long as the revolution is presented as something for the public domain, people will continue to have a private and a public mode of behaviour. We women are trapped in a private domain which represses us. For feminists, the personal is political and that's the way we'll break down these divisions in society and in the revolution.

Why hasn't the Nicaraguan revolution managed to make feminism its own?

I think it's partly to do with ignorance and theoretical limitations, but it's also because the revolutionary movement in Nicaragua is completely *machista* and feminism challenges male privileges. Even when the men are fighting against class privileges of every kind, in their heart of hearts they are not prepared to give up their privileges, however revolutionary they might otherwise be.

Then how it is possible to be a feminist with minority support and yet put up with these restrictive conditions?

Let me tell you about my own experience. I've found my own route and I've ventured along it very deliberately, because that was the only way I could stop being tortured by the stigma of reaching a certain age and still not being married. There's a very strong social pressure weighing on us: 'You have to have a child, you're getting older and older and old women without children are nobodies'. Somehow you have to manage to live with the fact you're not going to have children because you don't want to have children and because you're satisfied with your work. There are women who pay a very high price for having made this choice. That's a major ideological problem.

Was the Sandinista women's movement timid and limited as a result of this?

I wouldn't say the female leadership of AMNLAE had no conception of feminism but they didn't argue their case very well or perhaps weren't convinced themselves and didn't want to provoke any antagonism with the revolutionary *machismo*. This reflects the relationship of dependence between AMNLAE and the *macho* men of the FSLN. It wasn't unique to AMNLAE; it was characteristic of all FSLN organisations. Social forces enabled them to develop but new ideas on things like feminism fell on deaf ears among narrow-minded Sandinistas. Really, it was the party leadership's responsibility to understand this phenomenon, discuss it and to draw up coherent programmes accordingly.

Did your argument with the then President, Daniel Ortega, in 1987 at the women's 'de cara al pueblo' *meeting[1] have something to do with this?*

This incident showed how much he reacted personally as a man.

What actually happened?

A few women proposed points which in our opinion ought to have been included as women's demands at the constituent assembly. But the vast majority made demands for electricity and clean water. I felt these were issues for the community organisations or the trade unions, whereas the women's assembly ought to concern itself with issues like abortion which is the second most frequent cause of death for women in our country. But no one dared raise this except me. The problem of sexual discrimination in the workplace, sexual harassment, legislation concerning rape, indecent assault and abuse and a whole load of other serious problems in this country were all excluded from the discussion. I wanted to introduce them, but it wasn't possible.

Daniel Ortega reproached you for being 'petty bourgeois'. How did you take that?

I was surprised because Comandante Ortega was always very diplomatic in his dealings with people at assemblies and he said it to humiliate me, as if abortion wasn't at all an issue for the general population. He used my class origins as a stick to beat me with. But on the other hand, his behaviour didn't surprise me. His rejection of my views which that sort of approach aroused in him is typical of men, whether they're presidents or peasants. They react by reeling off what their culture has put into their heads. But they're just products of their environment. I don't mean to excuse Ortega in saying this, but I do understand how he could react in such an insulting way.

Isn't there a danger that feminist consciousness could overlook class consciousness?

Yes, there is. We need to maintain both types of consciousness. If the revolution aims to change and improve people's lives and if national liberation means the liberation of all repressed sectors of society, then you can't make a revolution while half the population are repressed by virtue of their sex. You can't pretend that their ideas are crazy. I think that trivialising this point seriously undermines the authority of our revolutionary ideas.

What's the difference between revolutionary machismo *and the* machismo *of the right?*

When it comes to *machismo*, all men are the same. *Machismo* is the most reactionary expression of any culture. Men are *macho* regardless of the political party they may belong to. I've heard well-known revolutionaries say that a woman's place is in the home, just as if they were the most reactionary old traditionalists. They say it without even realising they are talking total rubbish.

Feminists and left-wing women don't seem to have much to do with one another.

They went their separate ways a few decades ago because the Left just carried on as before and continued to repress women. It took away their autonomy and used them; it saw them strictly as party employees who were there to serve coffee. When women talked of making their own revolution, they were bundled off the stage until they were sick of the whole thing and created their own movement just for themselves. It's different for Nicaraguan feminists because we are all Sandinistas. The Left has betrayed the feminist movement worldwide, partly by reducing everything to economic principles, which have dominated left-wing thought, and partly by embracing Stalinism which has influenced all parties to a greater or lesser extent. So women have had a stark choice to make; either be a feminist or join the Left. The Left did not recognise that the two could go together.

How do feminists see their struggle with the right-wing government?

The fact that two women are in power doesn't mean that the interests of women are safe. We have Mrs Violeta de Chamorro and Miriam Arguello here, one president of the republic, the other of the national assembly. But they're women from the Right, conservatives. There's now a major drive to restore right-wing morality and force women back into hearth and home mainly to keep the few jobs which still exist for men.

Was it better to have a machista *revolutionary in power than a woman of the right?*

Of course. At least we could negotiate with him, convince, persuade him, politicise him and make him more aware; there was a space for discussion. But irrespective of the actual election result, we have to continue waging these struggles. The FSLN is conducting an internal debate which shows their ability to criticise themselves. Meanwhile, the rise of such a stupid and middle-aged right with all their technocratic thinking will be an incentive for us modern-thinking people to make a stand for social progress and for a revolution which will be for the good of all of us, right down to the very last moment of our lives. The alternative is to sell your soul and, whatever happens, I'll never do that.

Footnotes

[1] '*Cara al pueblo*' 'face the people', was a regular public event in which members of the Sandinista government made themselves available to questions from the public. These events were often broadcast on television.

Acronyms

AMNLAE *Asociación de Mujeres Nicaraguenses 'Luisa Amanda Espinosa'*
Luisa Amanda Espinoza Nicaraguan Women's Association

APRA *Alianza Popular Revolucionaria Americana*
Peruvian Aprista Party

ATC *Asociación de Trabajadores del Campo*
Agricultural Workers' Union (Nicaragua)

CETM *Centro de Estudios y Trabajo de la Mujer*
Women's Studies and Employment Centre (Bolivia)

CIDEM *Centro de Información y Documentación para la Mujer*
Women's Information and Documentation Centre (Bolivia)

CNM *Coordinadora Nacional de la Mujer*
National Women's Commission (Panama)

COB *Central Obrera Boliviana*
Central Organisation of Bolivian Workers

CONAMUS *Coordinadora Nacional de las Mujeres Salvadoreñas*
National Coordinating Committee of Women in El Salvador

CONAMU *Consejo Nacional de Mujeres*
National Women's Council (Uruguay)

CONAVIGUA *Coordinadora Nacional de Viudas de Guatemala*
National Coordinating Committee of Guatemalan Widows

CST *Central Sandinista de Trabajadores*
Sandinista Trade Union Confederation

CUT *Central Unitaria de Trabajadores*
Colombian Trade Union Confederation

CUT *Central Unitaria de Trabajadores*
Paraguayan Trade Union Confederation

FMLN *Frente Farabundo Martí para la Liberación Nacional*
Farabundo Martí liberation movement (El Salvador)

FSLN *Frente Sandinista de Liberación Nacional*
Sandinista Front for National Liberation (Nicaragua)

ILET	*Instituto Latinoamericano de Estudios Transnacionales* Latin American Institute for the Study of Transnationals
IMF	International Monetary Fund
IU	*Izquierda Unida* United Left (Peru)
MCP	*Movimiento Campesino Paraguayo* Paraguayan Peasants' Movement
NGOs	non-governmental organisations
PAN	*Partido de Acción Nacional* Party of National Action (Mexico)
PPC	*Partido Popular Cristiano* Popular Christian Party (Peru)
PRD	*Partido de la Revolución Democrática* Revolutionary Democratic Party (Mexico)
PRI	*Partido Revolucionario Institucional* Institutional Revolutionary Party (Mexico)
PRT	*Partido Revolucionario de Trabajadores* Revolutionary Worker's Party (Mexico)
SOFA	*Solidarité Fanm Ayisyen* Haitian Women's Solidarity

Resources and Action

UK

Action Aid funds a credit scheme for women in El Salvador's informal sector and an adult literacy scheme in Peru of which women are the main beneficiaries.
Hamlyn House, Highgate Hill, London N19 5PG

Aqui Nosotras is a Europe-wide network of Latin American women and European women working in solidarity with Latin America. It aims to improve co-ordination amongst Latin American women's initiatives in Europe and to promote an exchange of information about women's situation in Latin America.
Co-ordinated in Britain by Erika Paez c/o LAWRS (see below).

CAFOD (Catholic Fund for Overseas Development) supports mobilisation, networking and training of grassroots rural and urban women's organisations throughout Latin America. Recent campaigns have included 'Latin America. Land, Hope ..and Glory?' and refugees.
2 Romero Close, Stockwell Rd, London SW9 9TY

Central America Women's Network aims to provide a platform for Central American women in Britain through a newsletter, public meetings, and fundraising events.
c/o Helen Collinson, Latin America Bureau

Christian Aid gives priority to independent women's organisations in rural areas and in poor districts of cities throughout Latin America. Recent campaigns have highlighted women's working conditions in the Brazil nut and Colombian flower industries.
PO Box 100 London SE1 7RT

Latin American Women's Rights Service (LAWRS) offers advice to Latin American women in Britain on their immigration status, accommodation, health, benefits, employment, domestic violence, and legal rights.
The London Women's Centre, Wesley House, Wild Court, London WC2 5AV

One World Action supports a range of women-centred projects in the South, including several in Nicaragua and runs an education programme on gender, rights and development.
Floor 5, Weddel House, 13-14 West Smithfield, London EC1A 9HY

Oxfam aims to strengthen women's organisations throughout Latin America at both grassroots and national levels, and to encourage project partners in all spheres to include gender issues in their planning. Oxfam's Gender and Development Unit maintains links with many Latin American women's organisations.
274 Banbury Rd, Oxford OX2 7DZ

Save the Children Fund has programmes in Brazil, Peru, Honduras and the Caribbean. Key priority areas are support for organisations working on children's rights, educational and community projects and HIV/Aids prevention.
17 Grove Lane, London SE5 8RD

SCIAF (Scottish International Aid Fund) supports women's initiatives across Latin America and engages in constant dialogue with all its partners there to further understanding of gender issues. Project partners include CONAVIGUA in Guatemala.
5 Oswald St, Glasgow G1 4QR

SEAD (Scottish Education and Action for Development) researches, campaigns, and produces publications on development from a uniquely Scottish perspective. It has compiled case studies on natural childbirth in Nicaragua, mental health in Chile, and women organising in Mexico.
23 Castle St, Edinburgh EH2 3DN

Trocaire funds women's projects throughout Latin America, including community kitchens in Peru and domestic workers' groups in Colombia. It has also developed links between Irish trade unions and the Domestic Workers Union in Brazil.
169 Booterstown Ave, Co Dublin, Ireland

War on Want supports women's projects in Nicaragua, Brazil, and Chile. Its current educational campaign is 'A Human Right to Development', emphasising the rights of women, indigenous peoples, and workers.
Fenner Brockway House, 37-39 Great Guildford St, London SE1 OES

Womankind supports women's own initiatives in developing countries to gain access to training and education, credit, better health, freedom from violence and to improve their organisational effectiveness. In the UK Womankind raises awareness of women's concerns and their contributions to their communities. Grants range from a well women clinic in Peru to a literacy project for peasant farmers in Nicaragua and training for women trade unionists in Bolivia.
122 Whitechapel High St, London E1 7PT

USA

American Friends Service Communities support women's organizations in several Latin American countries in areas of leadership development, health, workers' rights and sexual minority rights.
1501 Cherry Street, Philadelphia PA 19003

Inter-American Commission of Women is an advisory body to the Organization of American States. It seeks to promote women's rights, their access to education, and their participation in economic and social development.
Organisation of American States, Washington DC, 20006

International Center for Research on Women undertakes policy research on women's economic and social status in Latin America.
1717 Massachusetts Ave, NW Suite 302, Washington DC 20036

NACLA (North American Congress on Latin America) carries out research on the political economy of the Americas. Its bi-monthly magazine, *Report on the Americas* contains regular articles and features on women.
475 Riverside Drive, Suite 454, New York, NY 10115. UK subscriptions: Latin America Bureau

WOLA (Washington Office on Latin America) informs US policymakers and educates the US public on conditions in Latin America. It has lobbied on women's human rights.
110 Maryland Ave, NE #404, Washington DC 20002-5696

Index

Further Reading

Women in Brazil
Caipora Women's Group, with an introduction by Sue Branford

'The real heroes in traditionally *macho* societies are often the women. The courage and hope of the women in this inspiring portrait of Brazil show that they are no exception.' Jan Rocha, *Guardian* Brazil correspondent

Tourist images of samba and bikinis mask the extreme poverty which wracks Brazil's shanty towns and peasant villages and causes untold misery to the women who live there.

But Brazilian women are fighting back. Over the last twenty years they have developed a myriad of grassroots organisations to resist discrimination: shanty town neighbourhood groups, Christian base communities, peasant associations, trade unions, women's and feminist movements.

In a mosaic of articles, poems, songs and testimonies, **Women in Brazil** paints an evocative picture of life for women in the world's most unequal society. Through the eyes of the women themselves, it disentangles and analyses the overlapping forms of discrimination imposed by *machismo*, racism, and exploitation at work.

1993   140 pages   ISBN 0 906156 79 3 (pbk)   £5.99 plus 61p p&p

Out of the Shadows: Women, Resistance and Politics in Latin America
Jo Fisher

'We'd lost so much in those years. It wasn't enough for things to go back to how they were before the dictatorship, we wanted something better.'
Ana Maria (Argentina)

Military rule in the 1970s and 1980s transformed women's lives across South America. With the systematic repression of the traditional, male-dominated left, a political vacuum appeared which women moved to fill. Coming together in communal kitchens, trade unions, relatives of the disappeared or as landless peasants, they challenged the very fabric of military rule with their new forms of resistance.

Out of the Shadows tells the story of women's fight against the generals in Argentina, Chile, Paraguay and Uruguay. Vivid firsthand accounts interspersed with Jo Fisher's sensitive analysis reveal the dramatic personal changes which resistance provoked. As they left the isolation of home life, women became aware of discrimination at the hands of their partners as well as the state. In the process, a new grassroots feminism was born.

'A fascinating and vivid insight into the rise of the independent women's movement in South America.' Maxine Molyneux, University of London

1993 200 pages with index ISBN 0 906156 77 7 (pbk) £7.99 plus 81p p&p